Twayne's United States Authors Series

EDITOR OF THIS VOLUME

Warren French

Indiana University

John Cheever

TUSAS 335

JOHN CHEEVER

By LYNNE WALDELAND
Northern Illinois University

TWAYNE PUBLISHERS
A DIVISION OF G. K. HALL & CO., BOSTON

Copyright © 1979 by G. K. Hall & Co.

Published in 1979 by Twayne Publishers,
A Division of G. K. Hall & Co.
All Rights Reserved

Printed on permanent/durable acid-free paper and bound
in the United States of America

Frontispiece photo of John Cheever by Nancy Crampton

Library of Congress Cataloging in Publication Data

Waldeland, Lynne.
John Cheever.

(Twayne's United States authors ; TUSAS 335)
Bibliography: p. 151–57
Includes index.
1. Cheever, John. 2. Authors, American—20th
century—Biography. I. French, Warren G., 1922–
PS3505.H6428Z94   1979   813'.5'2 [B]   78–26596
ISBN 0-8057-7251-0

For my mother and father

Contents

About the Author

Lynne Waldeland was born and educated in Minnesota, receiving her B.A. from St. Olaf College. She received her Master's degree and her Ph.D. from Purdue University. She taught at Albion College in Michigan and since 1970 has been an assistant professor at Northern Illinois University where she teaches American literature. She has published on Wright Morris, like John Cheever a contemporary American writer of fiction.

Her interest in Cheever stems from her fondness for the short story form, an appreciation for the novel of manners, and the sort of immoderate love of New England settings often found among those raised in the Midwest — all of which have been satisfied by Cheever's work throughout his career.

Preface

To write a critical book on the work of a living author is problematic. One eagerly awaits the writer's next book in the full knowledge that it could invalidate any generalizations or conclusions which the critic has had the temerity to draw. On the other hand, if the writer is good, then his or her work deserves serious critical attention during his or her lifetime, rather than after the career is safely wrapped up.

There is no question that the work of John Cheever is deserving of serious critical attention. His is a unique voice in mid-twentieth-century American fiction. He combines careful observation and an evocation of the way we live with a willingness to discern and celebrate human possibilities and the brightness and the beauty of life. Along with the contributions of his individual talent, he stands in a clear relationship to the American literary tradition. He has Emerson's faith in the potential for greatness of human beings and Thoreau's careful eye and love for the beauty of the natural world. He possesses a Hawthornesque awareness of the intricacies of human psychology and a Jamesian understanding of the interplay between the manners and the inner motives of human life. He shares with Hemingway a sense of the sudden and ironic shifts in our fortunes which test our mettle, sometimes strengthening us and sometimes ending in our destruction. He resembles Fitzgerald in his careful observation of the artifacts of our lives and in his willingness to express in lyric style and unashamed authorial presence his sense of the beauty of the world and the possibilities of the sensitive human being.

In a letter to critic Elizabeth Hardwick published in the *New York Review of Books,* Cheever wrote what might be considered a small manifesto on his sense of the possibilities of the novel in the contemporary world:

That the complexities of contemporary life have overwhelmed the novel would be claimed only by someone who knew nothing of the history of the novel and of the novel's dependence upon change.... That it is man's nature to be nostalgic we know, and the opportunities for nostalgia are abundant, but we can no longer, for example, claim to be disconcerted by the world of airports. . . . I think not that the novel has been overwhelmed by the complexities of contemporary life; I think the novel is the only art form we possess that has approached any mastery of this storm.

Cheever's work reveals that he has dealt honestly with the complexities of his times without escaping into nostalgia, fantasy, or simplistic social satire. That his times have sent him, personally and philosophically, difficult, painful, and complicated materials to work with will become clear in this book on his career. But from the beginning to the publication of *Falconer,* where he writes most directly of the punishing capacity of life in our time, Cheever, fully acknowledging that we are all living in a storm, has achieved mastery of that storm through the careful application of his considerable art.

Acknowledgments

My colleague MarySue Schriber aided me in this project from beginning to end, first in discussion of the fictional issues involved in Cheever's work and possible approaches to them and then by reading the entire manuscript. Any lapses in substance or style which occur in my work slipped by despite her vigilance; much that is solid or felicitous appears because of it. Another colleague, Rosalie Hewitt, also discussed Cheever's work with me and in other ways encouraged the completion of this project.

Northern Illinois University and its Department of English granted me a research leave for the spring semester, 1978, which allowed me to finish this book.

Most obviously, my book wouldn't exist if it were not for John Cheever and his fiction. His work has given me as much pleasure as that of any contemporary writer, a pleasure which did not diminish during the rigors of writing this book. Despite his power to make my work obsolete with the very next book he publishes, I look forward to that next book — and more — with great anticipation.

Chronology

My Next Novel; moved to Ossining, New York.

1964 *The Wapshot Scandal; The Brigadier and the Golf Widow;* spent six weeks in the USSR as part of a cultural exchange program; subject of *Time* magazine cover story (March 27).

1965 Howells Medal of the American Academy of Arts and Letters for *The Wapshot Scandal.*

1968 Film, *The Swimmer,* based on a Cheever short story, adapted and directed by Frank and Eleanor Perry (Columbia Pictures, May 15).

1969 *Bullet Park.*

1973 *The World of Apples;* elected to the American Academy of Arts and Letters.

1974 Writer-in-residence, University of Iowa.

1975 Writer-in-residence, Boston University.

1977 *Falconer; Newsweek* cover story (March 14).

1978 *The Stories of John Cheever*

CHAPTER 1

Cheever's Life and Early Work

IN its special Bicentennial issue, *Newsweek* asked prominent Americans in many professions to comment on their sense of where the country stood in its 200th year and what they could predict for its future. Designated to speak as The Novelist, John Cheever impatiently brushed aside suggestions of America's decay and decline as well as all questions phrased in the negative, such as "Do you think things will get worse?" He asserted instead that "there is still a newness in this country, a freshness. We are still experimenting. This is a haunted nation. Haunted by a dream of excellence."[1] He could as easily have been speaking of his own approach to his chosen vocation, writer of fiction. Throughout his career, he has celebrated what is new and fresh in our culture; he has experimented with ways to communicate his vision; and he has valued excellence, both in his own craft and as a capacity of humankind and of American culture.

Apparently, Cheever never seriously considered any work in life but writing. He claims he began to write at the age of six and that he was an accomplished raconteur in his progressive grade school. When he was just seventeen, the *New Republic* published his first story, "Expelled," based on his ignominious departure from prep school. His next story wasn't published until he had reached the advanced age of twenty-one; since then, he has steadily produced stories and novels marked by their artistic distinction and their perceptive view of American culture.

Despite this consistent record of productivity, rewarded as it has been with a National Book Award, major writers' fellowships and other awards, Cheever has not received enough serious critical attention, considering the quality and range of his work. Most of his novels and short-story collections have received favorable reviews upon publication, and he has even achieved best-seller status with several of his books. But as John Aldridge said in 1966,

"Cheever is one of the most grievously underdiscussed important writers we have at the present time,"[2] a situation which unfortunately hasn't changed much since the observation was made. Various reasons have been offered for this relative critical neglect: that he writes too much for the *New Yorker;* that he has been vaguely out-of-step with the prevailing winds of his time, for instance, celebrating tradition at a time when its force seems to be dissipating; that he is a "mere" chronicler of manners or that, on the contrary, he engages too much in fantasy and moral fable. Whatever the reasons for Cheever's receiving such little attention from serious critics, the scope and quality of his fiction requires that he be more appreciated as a writer who illuminates the culture in which he has lived and worked and as a craftsman who has made important contributions to the genre of fiction.

Because Cheever has chosen to locate his stories and novels in a recognizable American historical and social setting, an understanding of his background is useful if one is fully to appreciate his work. He was born in Quincy, Massachusetts, in 1912, and grew up there. He is descended on his father's side from an old New England seafaring family whose records go back to the Revolution. His grandfather was the last Cheever to go to sea; his father, Frederick Lincoln Cheever, owned a shoe factory until he was wiped out in the 1929 stock-market crash. His mother, an Englishwoman who had emigrated with her parents, opened a gift shop and became the primary supporter of the family. This family background has influenced Cheever's work in some visible ways. Clearly he is a product of the New England genteel tradition in which he was raised, with its sense of a workable moral code and its emphasis on cultural and artistic achievement. The union of these elements is exemplified in an anecdote Cheever recounts about the day he informed his parents of his wish to be a writer. As he remembers it, "After a couple of days they said that I could be a writer as long as I didn't seek wealth or fame."[3] Another less happy effect of his early family life grows out of his awareness of his parents' unhappy marriage and the tensions within it about work and success. Like Scott Fitzgerald, Cheever's childhood provided him with a firsthand view of the sort of failure of nerve which a business reversal can precipitate in a man who prides himself on supporting his family; in the case of Cheever's father, it was exacerbated by his wife's success in the world of business and her growing emotional independence. Cheever, more sympathetic to his father, left home early. He says: "I remained deeply disconcerted by the harm my mother's working did to my father's self-esteem,"[4] and readers of Cheever will surely recognize the form which that reaction took in his portrayals of Leander and Sarah in *The Wapshot Chronicle.* This old-fashioned, even chauvinistic, view of the proper relationship between the sexes has, however, changed somewhat for Cheever. In a recent interview, he commented on the situation of his parents and his own attitude:

He was a self-made man from a ruined, seafaring family, and suddenly he found himself helpless, unable to support his family. He tried to kill himself. She, on the other hand, was ecstatic to be independent. I didn't understand it at all. But today for me to grant what I think of as sovereignty to other men and women is one of the most thrilling experiences I know, and when I finally realized that my mother, managing her gift shop, felt herself to be sovereign, I was happy to get the news.[5]

This interest in the question of power in relationships between men and women, growing out of his own family situation, has remained a major theme in Cheever's work and has, of course, made his work particularly relevant in the last decade as the whole culture has focused on that issue.

Another important family relationship for Cheever was that with his older brother, Fred, who died in 1976. Cheever has been comparatively reticent on the subject of his brother, and readers' curiosity about that relationship is understandably piqued by the occurrences of fratricidal tensions, in such fictional works of Cheever's as "Good-by, My Brother," "The Low-Boy," and *Falconer.* John Cheever and his brother were apparently close; they left home together and shared quarters in Boston until John left alone for New York, a situation which seems to provide the inspiration for an early story, "The Brothers." Cheever once referred to this relationship as a "Siamese situation;"[6] in a more expansive vein he delineated it thus: "...the strongest love — not the most exciting or the richest or the most brilliant — but the strongest love of my life was for my brother."[7] He also confesses, in the same interview in which he commented on his love for his brother, that he once contemplated killing him. He has not chosen to elaborate further on this relationship, but it is clear from his fiction that, along with that with his parents, it has been crucial in his life.

Cheever's formal education ended abruptly at the age of seven-

teen when he was expelled from Thayer Academy, in South Brain-
tree, Massachusetts, not the sort of development one would expect
in the life of someone who has seemingly absorbed the Calvinist
bent of his New England heritage. He attributes the bad behavior
which led to his expulsion to his growing awareness of the dimensions of his parents' unhappiness and to his sense that Thayer was
more interested in placing its students at Harvard than in providing
them with real educations. From this vantage point, it is hard to see
what must have seemed then a calamity as anything but a fortunate
mishap for Cheever, for it gave him both inspiration and leisure to
turn his energies to fiction. The immediate result was his first published story, accepted for the October 1, 1930, issue of the *New
Republic* by no less a reader than Malcolm Cowley. The long-term
effect was that Cheever, except for a stint in the army during World
War II, has avoided any structure, educational or vocational, that
wasn't conducive to his work as a writer.

It was, of course, a coup for a seventeen-year-old to have his first
story accepted by so prestigious a magazine. What is perhaps more
surprising is the tone of the story itself; written as it was in the emotional wake of a traumatic experience, even for a disinclined stu-
dent, the story avoids such predictable emotions as bitterness,
extensive self-justification, or self-pity. The story does dramatize
the hypocrisy of the institution's educational goals, as Salinger
would do at more length in *The Catcher in the Rye,* and it does indicate the protagonist's sense of the wrench in his life caused by this
event, foreshadowing Sammy's awareness at the end of Updike's
"A & P." But the story is primarily interesting for its careful and
gentle rendering of characters. There is the retired colonel called
upon to speak at an assembly who, instead of mouthing inspiring
slogans about war, breaks into tears at the memory of young men
like those seated before him who died on battlefields. There is the
English teacher whose distinction is to have seen *Hamlet* twenty-
seven times and to have taught it for sixteen years; she is consequently "a sort of immortal" whose added usefulness is that *her*
interpretation is the one accepted on college-board exams. In the
last section of the story, "Five Months Later," the narrator
acknowledges that it is particularly hard to leave a place for bad
reasons, such as anger and frustration, and that he feels oddly isolated at having no place to which he must report at 9:00 A.M. each
day. He ends: "I am not sorry. I am not at all glad."[8] Structurally
or stylistically, the story is not very indicative of the artistry that

will mark Cheever's work to come. But, in addition to its simple historical interest as the first published story of an important writer, "Expelled" does foreshadow some soon-to-be-developed strengths, such as an accurate ear for language and an interest in the revealing details of individual lives.

After his expulsion from prep school, Cheever went on a walking tour of Europe with his brother and then settled in Boston, where he was subsidized by his brother while he wrote. Here he was befriended by members of an intellectual group, including Hazel Hawthorne and Henry Wadsworth Longfellow Dana, a drama professor at Harvard. Soon Cheever moved to New York City and lived in a room on Hudson Street so extreme in its air of poverty that Walker Evans immortalized it in a photograph. Cheever has said very little about these years, but we know that he did spend some time at Yaddo, the writer's colony in Saratoga Springs, New York, where he did odd jobs to support himself. He also worked briefly in the New York City story department of MGM writing synopses and taught composition at Barnard College, finally ending up in the army during World War II. These were primarily years of learning his craft, years when he seems to have been a full-time observer of life around him in the city, storing up incidents, lines of dialogue, and other details which would later appear in his stories.

In 1941, he married Mary M. Winternitz, the daughter of a long-established Connecticut family, whose father was the Dean of the Yale Medical School. Cheever was fascinated by her huge, close-knit family and became close to his in-laws, especially to Mary's father, just as his wife was trying to effect some necessary distance from home and family. The Cheevers have three children and a marriage that Cheever himself has called "extraordinary." Both his fiction and his comments in interviews reveal that he is no sentimentalist about the enduringness of love. He explains the success of his own marriage in a magazine interview conducted by his daughter: "That two people of our violent temperament have been able to live together for nearly forty years as we have seems to me a splendid example of the richness and diversity of human nature ... and in this forty years there's scarcely been a week in which we haven't planned to get a divorce."[9] Obviously Cheever sees most successful human relationships as surviving on sustained efforts of will and imagination. Marriage and family relationships are perhaps his most frequently chosen subjects, and it is clear throughout his fiction that Cheever has drawn extensively upon his experience as husband and father, just as he has made use of his experiences as son and brother.

Cheever's career spans almost five decades of American cultural history. Too young to have experienced World War I personally and aware of the Depression primarily from observing its effects on his father, these events play a comparatively small role in his work. However, he doesn't make much more direct use of later events in our history which he did experience personally. World War II does not play a major role in his work, although it is the general subject of several stories from the early 1940s. The Korean and Vietnam wars are barely mentioned. No 1930s-style flirtation with communism is evident in his stories, nor is there a catastrophic sense of life under the threat of a mushroom-shaped cloud, except for a story about the bomb-shelter paranoia of the 1950s, ''The Brigadier and the Golf Widow.'' Some sense of these events of American history comes through in the stories, but it almost always functions as a backdrop for the real subject of his work — the characters' interactions with each other and with the daily challenges of their lives, from commuter trains to zoning restrictions to divorces to job transfers to country-club dances to nervous breakdowns. Cheever is often called a moralist, a label which is inaccurate if it suggests a tendency to subordinate the fictional elements of his stories to some didactic, thematic statement but a designation which makes sense if it means that Cheever is almost always interested in the character, the moral fiber even, of the human beings who populate his fictional world.

I   The Way Some People Live *(1943)*

The work of Cheever's in which the historical context is most strongly invoked is his first collection of short stories, *The Way Some People Live,* published in 1943. From 1930, the year of his first story, to 1943, Cheever published more than forty stories, thirty of which appear in this volume. To have such a collection published, during wartime and in the absence of an attention-getting novel to his credit, was no mean feat. It attests, in part, to the greater esteem in which the short story was held in the 1930s and 1940s than now. Then mass-circulation magazines gave much more space to their publication than they have since. But the publication attests also to the seriousness with which Cheever's early work was taken. The title of the collection is aptly chosen; the focus of most of the stories is on a realistic rendering of human experiences, sometimes in relation to the historical and cultural circumstances of the 1930s and early 1940s and sometimes in terms of more universal human dilemmas and concerns.

The fact of World War II is the most dominant historical note in this collection; it serves to provide either a backdrop or the central situation of eight of the stories. In "The Survivor," it is important only as background; a man bores others in a bar with the tale of his escape from a German torpedo. In "A Border Incident," the suspicion about Germans and the fact that some Germans were interned in camps in Canada forms part of the story's situation. In other stories the war is more central, but none of them involves combat; rather, they focus on young men celebrating before their induction ("These Tragic Years"), the financial hardships of wives left behind ("The Shape of a Night"), the mixture of exhilaration and regret which accompanies a life-change like entering the army ("Goodby Broadway — Hello, Hello" and "The Man Who Was Very Homesick for New York"), and the conflict between the world back home and the new realities of army life, which is the subject of the best of the war-related stories, "Problem No. 4." In this story, a new soldier's letter to his wife back home ("I don't really have much use for a dressing gown here") is juxtaposed with the man's participation in war games, in which one officer tells him he has been killed and another informs him he was adequately concealed and escaped death. The effect of the story is to emphasize the remoteness of the civilian life which the soldier has left behind as well as the irrelevance of the training he is receiving in boot camp.

The Depression also serves as the backdrop for several stories, most importantly "Run, Sheep, Run," in which a decent man robs a bookstore of a few dollars so that he can take his wife on an outing in the country, and "The Law Of the Jungle," in which a son who is financially able plans to buy back his parents' home from the bank and invites them to live there with him, his wife, and their projected family. His mother is delighted at this restoration of her former home and status, but his father is opposed and desperately pleads with his son to save his money, postpone starting a family, and not buy the house. The father has been traumatized by having been prosperous and then having lost everything and has retreated into a self-defensive shell into which he wishes to pull his son as well.

Marxism makes one brief, relatively undeveloped appearance in the volume in the story "The New World." One of several stories in this volume which involve a conflict between brothers, this one features an older brother who has assimilated the values of his conservative, traditional family, and a younger one, who is persuaded of the decadence of that way of life and who announces that if drafted he will refuse to fight for the system of social order that means so much to his family.

Many of the stories in *The Way Some People Live* make some claim on our attention largely because of some vivid word-pictures of characters, settings, or human reactions to situations. Most of the reviewers singled out "Of Love: A Testimony" as the best story in the volume. Essentially a story about an unconventional love triangle, it is, perhaps, the most innovative in form, with a high degree of authorial commentary mingled with forays into the consciousness of the main characters. But aside from this experimentation with point of view, the story is essentially static, a problem almost predictable in the light of the title. Since the relationships change, the story requires a more dynamic narrative line than it is given; as it is, it resembles a series of film freeze-frames, and we are finally left musing philosophically about the nature of love rather than curiously about the characters' motivations and actions.

My own choice as the volume's most distinguished story is "The Brothers," only the fifth story Cheever published. It is interesting not only in itself but also as the first in what will become a long line of stories dealing with fraternal relationships. The story, which is slightly reminiscent of de Maupassant's "Two Little Soldiers," involves brothers who are not hostile rivals but rather extraordinarily close, having drawn together in an intense, self-protective relationship after the bitter divorce of their parents. They live together and share all their spare-time activities so that the structure of their lives finally has the effect of excluding the rest of the world. The extent of this exclusivity doesn't become apparent — and then only to one of them — until a girl falls in love with one of the brothers. Kenneth, the object of this affection, is totally oblivious to it, but his brother Tom notices not only the girl's feelings but also his brother's complacent insensitivity to them. Gradually, Tom is led to question the health of a relationship which so completely shuts out the rest of the world. Aware that his brother would not feel this to be a problem, Tom nevertheless decides to go away: "He felt a sharp thrust of responsibility for them both — they must live and not wear out their lives like old clothes, in a devotion that would defeat its own purpose'' (p. 173).[10] The purpose of this devotion was survival, but Tom realizes that they will have survived for nothing if they refuse to be nourished by the world. In the end, the girl moves on to a new interest, but the strategy for which she had been the catalyst begins to work on Kenneth and he begins to understand his brother's action:

Now he felt the pain that Tom had brought down on both of them without any indignation; they had tried to give their lives some meaning and order, and for love of the same world that had driven them together, they had had to separate. He walked through the fields, clutching involuntarily at the air, as if something were slipping from his grasp, and swearing and looking around him like a stranger at the new, strange, vivid world. (p. 175)

This affirmative ending may grow out of Cheever's desire to understand why he had left the security of the relationship he had with his own brother as well as the belief, to be reiterated throughout his fiction, that one must be open to all experience. This story does have the narrative movement and character development lacking in others in this anthology. It gains a particular tension from the differences in what each brother perceives. It is a polished and effective work of fiction.

The other unusually successful story in this volume is "Publick House." As in "The Brothers," Cheever here seems to draw directly on his own family experience to some degree, this time on his mother's running a gift shop. In the story Lincoln Briggs's mother has turned the family summer place into a restaurant and antique shop, disrupting the life of his grandfather, who bitterly observes that she is "selling the past." The family dines on elegant leftovers at unreasonable hours on a corner of the kitchen table, while Lincoln's mother goes through her well-rehearsed spiel about the age of the house and the distinguished visitors from Revolutionary times who have stayed there. Mrs. Briggs's attitude toward her business career is ambivalent. In an amusing letter in which she invites her son to come to the old family homestead for his vacation, maternal concern for his health and rest mingle with proud descriptions of her operation of the inn. At the end, however, when Lincoln and his mother are having a supper of leftover tea sandwiches, she suddenly commences her historical narrative but this time in a self-mocking tone, punctuated by admissions that she is worried about expenses and fatigued by her long hours; this business day ends with the mistress of the "Publick House" in tears. This story does not develop as fully as "The Brothers." There is an initial conflict between Mrs. Briggs's apparent satisfaction with her work and the resentment of her father and her son at the turning of their home into a place of business. But at the end we realize that there is an inner conflict in Mrs. Briggs herself, and with that revelation the story ends. The characters, especially Mrs. Briggs, are well drawn in this story, and the climax is dramatically handled.

One more story in this volume bears mention only because it seems to owe something in its conception to another famous story, Hemingway's "Cat in the Rain." In the Hemingway story, a woman empathizes with a wet cat in a storm, and the incident brings out her desire for a home, a family, and stability in her life. In Cheever's story, a couple is moving, and their cat escapes in the process. The woman is frantic, and after a futile search, the husband, to calm her, makes promises which suggest that the same things are missing in their marriage that the woman in Hemingway's story wished for. The husband promises that they can have a child, that they'll save money, stop drinking, buy a house, have a garden, that they won't live "like this" anymore. Then the cat turns up, and they drive off. It is a very slight, but well-told story, and one which seems to indicate one likely influence on Cheever's work.

On the whole, the stories in this book are adequate but not memorable. They seem, especially in relation to Cheever's later work, oddly static. Several consist entirely of conversations but without the tension and repressed feeling that make "mere" conversations in Hemingway the most active prose imaginable. Most of the stories are more like vignettes or sketches than fully developed narratives; in them, situations are delineated but not developed. The volume was, for the most part, favorably received by reviewers, though several faulted Cheever for a sort of monotony of subject and style. A few reviewers blamed the defects they saw in the volume on the fact that Cheever wrote the stories for magazines, especially the *New Yorker,* which was believed to impose a limiting formula on its fiction writers. Mark Schorer liked the stories well enough to wish that they had been better and suggests that the reason Cheever doesn't fully deliver on the promise implicit in some of the stories is that "he limits himself . . . to the conventions of magazine realism and the kind of statement that realism is capable of making."[11] This judgment seems essentially just, for the book is marked as apprenticeship work when one sees in later stories how far Cheever moves beyond the limited options of the realistic mode.

The Way Some People Live is important primarily as a book in which we can observe a writer learning his craft. In it we see Cheever taking possession of the experiences of his own life, as in "The Brothers" and "Publick House." The degree to which he was energized by working with his own background is made clear by the comparatively high quality of those stories. We also see the author in these stories assimilating the large cultural and historical events of his time and the daily details of personality, setting, and human situations that he observed. A respectable volume for a writer's first collected fiction, it would soon be overshadowed by the stories which were published in his next book, *The Enormous Radio and Other Stories*.

CHAPTER 2

The Enormous Radio:
Cheever's Short-Story Craft

BECAUSE John Cheever established himself first as a short-story writer and because he has continued to publish stories as well as novels throughout his career, his technique as a writer of short fiction has received a reasonable amount of critical attention. Critical response to his short works has run the gamut from its rejection as merely a successful execution of "the *New Yorker* story," thought by some critics to be a formulaic and trivial manifestation of fiction, to attempts really to delineate the particular achievement of his stories, especially as they combine disparate modes of storytelling. Although Cheever has considerably developed his craft since the publication of *The Enormous Radio and Other Stories* (1953), this collection of fourteen stories, all of which originally appeared in the *New Yorker,* serves as a useful introduction to the range and quality of Cheever's work in the short story form.

Since so much is made of it, Cheever's relationship to the *New Yorker* bears some attention. Katharine White, fiction editor for the magazine, accepted a story of Cheever's first in 1940, and since then, he has published more than 120 stories in the *New Yorker,* making him its most frequent contributor of fiction except for John O'Hara. The real question, however, is whether or not there is any such thing as a *"New Yorker* story," whether the magazine imposes a set of prerequisites, spoken or unspoken, which seriously limits an author's subject or style. Cheever seems to have no sense of having been governed by any such thing and expresses his sense of relationship to the magazine in practical terms: "I never wrote for The New Yorker and I never stopped writing for The New Yorker — they bought my stories."[1] His sense of connection to the long-time editor Harold Ross is more personal; Cheever has referred to Ross as a sort of father figure, though he also points out that Ross's editing technique was occasionally brilliant, occasionally erratic. Cheever's sense was that Ross liked to keep the writer stirred up and yet to keep his own editorial hand in every stage of the publication process; Cheever's final judgment on his dealings with Ross indicates that "it was a creative, destructive relationship from which I learned a great deal, and I miss him."[2] Despite Cheever's denial that the magazine has a strict formula, there has been a tendency, strongest during the 1930s and early 1940s when the magazine was judged to possess too little social conscience, on the part of some reviewers and critics to apply what seems to be an *a priori* prejudice against the *New Yorker* to Cheever's fiction, perceiving in it limitations of range of interest and depth of feeling which are then attributed to his writing for the *New Yorker*. Clearly, this is not a useful critical tack; more to the point, the *New Yorker* aided Cheever's career in that it bought his stories consistently throughout the years, allowing him the opportunity to survive financially while he improved and refined his art. Of course, the magazine must have liked what he wrote, but this preference does not mean that it told him how to write.

The Enormous Radio and Other Stories shows a remarkable development beyond Cheever's previous achievements in *The Way Some People Live*. The very fact that the second volume contains only fourteen stories compared to thirty in its predecessor, although the two collections are nearly the same length, indicates that the later stories are more fully developed narratives. With a few exceptions, the stories in this collection are more complex in technique than the sketches of his earlier book, and they have a greater range of subject matter and setting. The stories in *The Way Some People Live* almost all employed urban settings, and most involved characters whose lives ran on city rhythms. In fact, those critics who simplistically refer to Cheever as a chronicler of the suburbs are overlooking the degree to which the city, especially New York, dominates his first collection and continues to be important in a number of stories in his second volume. In *The Enormous Radio,* however, Cheever also uses as settings a seaside cottage ("Goodby, My Brother"), a suburb ("The Cure"), a ski resort ("The Hartleys"), and a farm ("The Summer Farmer"). Almost the entire volume consists of stories more complex and more fully developed than his earlier work. Only "Christmas is a Sad Season for the Poor" and "Clancy in the Tower of Babel," both featuring elevator operators as protagonists, are reminiscent of the sketches that dominated the earlier volume. These are both fairly slight efforts, using the outsider status of the elevator operator in apartment buildings to comment on the manners and morals of the residents.

Three of the stories in this collection — "Goodby, My Brother," "Torch Song," and "The Enormous Radio" — are among the most frequently anthologized of Cheever's stories. They are deservedly famous for their effective and sometimes innovative storytelling and, consequently, provide a good point from which to begin to appreciate the development of Cheever's technique as it emerges in this volume. Cheever is seldom listed among the major innovators in fiction in the twentieth century, perhaps because much of his work seems at first glance to be quite traditional in form. But Walter Clemons perceptively observes that "long before Donald Barthelme, John Barth and Thomas Pynchon began tinkering with narrative conventions, Cheever had unobtrusively disrupted the expected shapes of fiction,"[3] and it is primarily in his short fiction, starting with the stories in this volume and particularly in these three stories, that this genre-expanding experimentation takes place.

The first, "Goodby, My Brother," is of interest because it deals with one of Cheever's most frequent subjects, family relationships, especially those between brothers. Comparison of this more complex story with "The Brothers" from the previous volume not only reveals that here Cheever takes a far more negative view of fraternal relationships, but also illuminates the change in his storytelling art. In this story the Pommeroy family has gathered at its summer home for a vacation. There is a comfortable relationship between the widowed mother and three of her four children, Diana, Chaddy, and the narrator, a second brother. The tranquillity of the family is disrupted by the arrival of a third brother, Lawrence, the youngest, who spends the visit pointing out the erosion of the sea wall, declining to participate in family tennis games or backgammon matches, ridiculing the country-club ball, and criticizing the life-styles and moral fiber of his mother and siblings. The narrator sees him as a throwback to earlier generations of Pommeroys who were Puritan ministers. He reflects:

The Pommeroys were ministers until the middle of the nineteenth century, and the harshness of their thought — man is full of misery, and all earthly beauty is lustful and corrupt — has been preserved in books and sermons. . . . If you are raised in this atmosphere . . . I think it is a trial of the spirit to reject its habit of guilt, self-denial, taciturnity, and penitence, and it seemed to me to have been a trial of the spirit in which Lawrence had succumbed. (p. 7)[4]

The story develops a distinction between Lawrence, the gloom-monger and doom-sayer, and the rest of the family, whose inheritance from tradition leads them to value the past, commit themselves to the present, and appreciate each other. Tensions build and culminate in a confrontation on the beach between Lawrence and the narrator. After a nasty argument, the narrator, in frustration, strikes Lawrence from behind with a heavy root he finds on the beach, in what almost seems to be a biblical reversal in which an Abel-figure strikes Cain. As he watches the blood darken his brother's hair, the narrator realizes: "Then I wished that he was dead, dead and about to be buried, not buried but about to be buried, because I did not want to be denied ceremony and decorum in putting him away, in putting him out of my consciousness..." (p. 25). The worst of his rage over, the narrator feels divided — part murderer, part good Samaritan — and he pulls Lawrence, who is not seriously injured, out of the undertow and binds his wound. Lawrence leaves the next day, and harmony is restored to the family.

The story ends with a monologue by the narrator, a favorite fictional device which we will see often in Cheever's work:

Oh, what can you do with a man like that? . . . How can you dissuade his eye in a crowd from seeking out the cheek with acne, the infirm hand; how can you teach him to respond to the inestimable greatness of the race, the harsh surface beauty of life; how can you put his finger for him on the obdurate truths before which fear and horror are powerless? The sea that morning was iridescent and dark. My wife and my sister were swimming — Diana and Helen — and I saw their uncovered heads, black and gold in the dark water. I saw them come out and I saw that they were naked, unshy, beautiful, and full of grace, and I watched the naked women walk out of the sea. (p. 27)

The mythical overtones here of goddesses appearing out of the sea as well as the cadences of the King James Bible which echo in the last sentence underline the story's point that traditions needn't be constricting but can be life-enhancing. Lawrence, preserving one aspect of the family heritage, is a Hawthornesque character — an

Ethan Brand ferreting out weakness and corruption in everything
he sees. But the narrator, also possessed of a proud sense of
lineage, valuing his cultural past and family ties, is able to perceive
"the greatness of the race" like Emerson and to respond joyfully to
"the harsh surface beauty of life" like Thoreau.

The other two stories, "Torch Song" and "The Enormous
Radio," are more innovative in their telling. The former involves a
mythic transformation of one of the characters; the latter centers
around a fantastic metamorphosis of an object in the story. "Torch
Song" begins with an ominous introduction of the character
involved:

> After Jack Lorey had known Joan Harris in New York for a few years,
> he began to think of her as The Widow. She always wore black, and he was
> always given the feeling, by a curious disorder in her apartment, that the
> undertakers had just left. This impression did not stem from malice on his
> part, for he was fond of Joan.... They came from the same city in
> Ohio.... They were the same age, and during their first summer in the
> city they used to meet after work and drink Martinis in places like the
> Brevoort and Charles.... (p. 97)

But Cheever keeps us off balance in a paragraph like the above; the
ominous hints are offset by the ordinary details of two friends
keeping in touch in the city. As the years go on, Jack keeps encountering Joan in restaurants, through the window of a train, sometimes at parties at her apartment. Through Jack's two marriages,
job changes, and army service, Joan reappears at lengthy intervals,
always with a different man, and always with men in some sort of
trouble: some are drunks, some are refugees, most are unem-
ployed. The men often abuse Joan; and, for much of the story, the
reader's sympathies are likely to be with her as a long-suffering
patroness of these lost souls. Even when Jack learns, as he frequently does in these reunions, that the last man she was with is
now dead or in some other way departed from the scene, he thinks
little of the recurrence of the pattern because Joan's patience and
good will seem boundless and healthy. It is not until Jack himself
loses his job and then becomes ill that he — and we — begin to see
what has really been happening. Joan shows up in his furnished
room, nurses him, and prepares to move in. Suddenly Jack, recall-
ing that all her former lovers are dead, sees her as a sort of Angel of
Death, who, smelling out the signs of decay, moves in like an emo-

tional vulture for the kill. He orders her out of his room, shouting, "Does it make you feel young to watch the dying? ... Is that the lewdness that keeps you young? Is that why you dress like a crow?" (p. 114). Joan serenely disregards this outburst and leaves for work with a promise to return in the evening. Jack frantically rises, dresses, gathers his belongings, and even empties the ashtrays and sweeps the floor with his shirt "so that there would be no trace of his life, of his body, when that lewd and searching shape of death came there to find him in the evening" (p. 114). One must, of course, ascertain whether or not it is only from Jack's fevered viewpoint that Joan appears to be an Angel of Death. The last line of the story, quoted above, seems to be authorial, though it could be from Jack's point of view. However, as one thinks back through the story, the events seem to bear out this interpretation. There has been a succession of men who have died, and their resentment and hostility toward Joan was similar to Jack's striking out at her when he feels her threatening presence. We have to presume, I think, that the last line is the author putting his stamp on the revelation of Joan's vampirish love of the dying. This story deals with a situation that does occur in everyday life, that of a person deriving a sense of usefulness by associating exclusively with the desperately needy; but here Cheever gives such a phenomenon a supernatural twist that raises the story from the level of a psychological case history to a sort of legendary realm. Joan's symbolic dressing in black, our gradual realization that all her men are dead, and her mysterious appearance in Jack's life at the moment when he is most vulnerable all give the story a sort of horror that makes it relatively easy to believe that we have read a story about an Angel of Death.

"The Enormous Radio" is probably the best story in the collection. It, too, is based on a fantastic premise, this one that a radio can mysteriously tune in the goings-on in other apartments in the building where the protagonists, Jim and Irene Westcott, live. The couple is portrayed as average in aspiration and achievement: "They were the parents of two young children, they had been married nine years, they lived on the twelfth floor of an apartment house near Sutton Place, they went to the theatre on an average of 10.3 times a year, and they hoped someday to live in Westchester" (p. 169). The only difference in their lives from those around them — and they conceal this difference — is that they are passionately interested in classical music. Ironically, it is their one unique trait that leads to the point of the story; Jim buys Irene a fancy new

radio when their old one breaks during a Schubert quartet. The new
radio is depicted ominously — much as Joan Harris was in "Torch
Song"; it has an ugly cabinet and stands among Irene's other fur-
nishings "like an intruder." When turned on, the complex dials
glow with "a malevolent green light"; it comes to life with a violent
roar of sound. Irene is made uneasy by this acquisition. As the
couple listens to the new radio, it not only plays music but picks up
a variety of discordant sounds — telephones, electric razors, cooking appliances. Finally, it transmits conversations in other apartments; Jim and Irene overhear marital quarrels, nurses reading
bedtime stories, tales of financial woes, revelations of dishonesty.
After prudently ascertaining that *they* cannot be heard, Jim and
Irene settle down for a fascinating evening of eavesdropping. Irene
even gets up in the middle of the night to listen some more. But in a
twist which is reminiscent of Hawthorne, Irene comes to be
haunted by all she has heard and begins to scan the faces of people
she meets in the elevator for signs of the dishevelment she has
learned exists in their private lives. Finally, distraught at these
revelations of hidden secrets, she begs her husband to assure her
that *their* lives are not like those around them. The radio, however,
which brought the knowledge of discord into their lives, has the
effect of stripping away the veneer that kept the same sort of discord at bay in their lives. Jim, worried about money, accuses his
wife of improvidence and then, in an angry outburst, reveals the
hidden secrets of their lives just as the radio has done for the
neighbors':

Why are you so Christly all of a sudden? What's turned you overnight into
a convent girl? You stole your mother's jewelry before they probated her
will. You never gave your sister a cent of that money that was intended for
her — not even when she needed it. You made Grace Howland's life miserable, and where was all your piety and your virtue when you went to that
abortionist? . . . (p. 180)

Desperately trying to shut out his words, Irene turns on the radio,
hoping to hear the Sweeneys' nurse crooning a comforting lullaby.
But, as her husband continues to shout, the voice on the radio,
"suave and noncommittal," announces railroad disasters, a fire in a
hospital for blind children, the temperature and the humidity. Irene
has to face her own moment of self-awareness and guilt with no
comfort — only a sense of the giddy motions of the world between

the cataclysmic and the mundane.

This story, with the radio droning on into the distance at the end, has an effective climax and is one of Cheever's most memorable. It has been viewed as a modern version of the Edenic myth with the radio acting as the serpent to Irene's Eve.[5] More helpfully, in my view, the story has been compared to Hawthorne's "Young Goodman Brown."[6] In this story, the plausibility of the radio's strange power is as insignificant in the end as is the issue in "Young Goodman Brown" of whether or not there really was a devil's bonfire in the forest. What is important is the effect upon the characters of what *they* believe has happened. Irene's preternatural sense of evil and unhappiness, following the radio's revelations, reminds us not only of Young Goodman Brown sensing evil everywhere in his community after his traumatic night but also of Hester Prynne, through her own suffering, becoming sensitive to the signs of hidden guilt and suffering in the faces she meets in *The Scarlet Letter.* One critic observes that "in Cheever's darker tales objects often seem to overwhelm the characters' sense of well-being, as if these people were living in a strange and alien world of obstacles and mysteriously laid traps."[7] Such a situation certainly informs "The Enormous Radio"; the effects of the radio overwhelm the characters' carefully constructed sense that they are not like other people, that they are more loving, less guilty. The story's narrative pace is fast, allowing for little slippage in the necessary suspension of disbelief that must take place in the reader for this story to work. And the abruptness of the ending is perfect, leaving us with the image of Irene standing, self-esteem in shreds, before the mysterious radio which, having destroyed her illusions, now perversely gives the news.

Most of the other stories in this collection are in some way concerned with people who do not quite belong in the world in which they are trying to live. In "The Pot of Gold" Ralph and Laura Whittemore are innocents in pursuit of wealth and success in the business world whose quest is doomed to repeated failure because of their incredibly bad luck and a degree of naiveté. In "O City of Broken Dreams" the cause of the characters' dislocation is more obvious. Evarts Malloy and his family have come from an Indiana small town to Manhattan on the strength of one act of a folksy play which Evarts has written and in which a down-on-his-luck producer has shown some interest. Duped during their stay by everyone from the hotel bellboy to several shyster agents and producers, they finally leave town, but, Cheever hints, probably not to return home where their stories might not be believed, but perhaps to remain on the train all the way to California, made permanent wanderers by their disillusionment. In "The Children" a couple, Victor and Theresa MacKenzie, spend their entire lives being surrogate children to a series of lonely but often cruel rich people. They are the sort of persons whom one automatically asks to mix the drinks or run errands; they do not, however, feel put upon but, rather, fulfilled by such exploitation and at home whenever they find themselves taken in by people who will use them in this way. "The Hartleys" are a couple who seem happy on the surface as they arrive at a ski resort with their daughter. However, we learn that they have been separated and that now, together again, they are engaged in frantically revisiting places where they had been happy in the past to try to recapture the feelings of that other time. The futility of this search turns to tragedy; their daughter is killed in an accident on the ski tow, a hostage to their ill-fated attempt to reestablish a meaningful relationship by reliving the past. "The Summer Farmer" involves a man who commutes on the weekends from his job in the city to a small farm, a place he loves immoderately. The story revolves around a conflict between this man, Paul Hollis, and Kasiak, a local farmer whom Paul hires to help with heavy chores and who taunts Paul about his outsider status by predicting that he will not return the following year. The tension between them is great enough so that when Paul's children's pet rabbits are poisoned, he accuses Kasiak of having left poison in the rabbit hutch with an eye toward hurting the children. It turns out that Paul's wife left the poison there the previous summer. Paul has to rush to catch the train back to the city after this trying weekend.

No harm had been done, he thought. "No harm," he said under his breath as he swung his suitcase onto the rack — a man of forty with signs of mortality in a tremor of his right hand, signs of obsoleteness in his confused frown, a summer farmer with blistered hands, a sunburn, and lame shoulders, so visibly shaken by some recent loss of principle that it would have been noticed by a stranger across the aisle. (p. 151)

The point of the story seems to be the difficulty of understanding and participating in an alternative way of life, a difficulty underlined by Paul's hypersensitivity to the hired man's prediction that he won't be back and by his sense of dislocation at the end of the story.

One story in the volume foreshadows the suburban stories which will dominate Cheever's next collection. "The Cure," set in an unnamed suburb, involves a couple whose marriage is rocky. The narrator's wife has just left him for what may be the final time; their previous separations have been serious, one ending in divorce and then remarriage. The narrator, accepting the finality of this last break, prepares himself for living alone, the loss of his house, and other disruptions while his wife and children are away at a summer place. One night a Peeping Tom comes and watches the narrator through the picture window, a visitation which is repeated several times even after the narrator recognizes the prowler as one of his neighbors. He becomes jumpy alone in the house, a state of mind compounded when a woman who claims to be clairvoyant tells him at a party that she sees a rope around his neck. That night, when the Peeping Tom returns, the narrator concludes that it's because he has some mysterious awareness that he is to witness a hanging. The narrator searches house and garage, finds the only piece of rope on the premises, and burns it. Caught up in visions of ropes, the narrator has an irrational urge the next day in the city to embrace a strange woman he sees on the street, believing that only such an act can save his life. That night, his wife calls, they are reconciled, and, we are told, they've been happy ever since. The Peeping Tom never returns, so that we are tempted to conclude that he was a sort of fortunate visitant, sent in to shock the narrator back to his senses so that he would put forth the effort necessary to make his marriage work. This mixture of everyday details with supernatural occurrences — or at least ominously weighty coincidences — plus the fortuitousness of the ending are qualities that will characterize the stories in Cheever's next collection, *The Housebreaker of Shady Hill.*

The Enormous Radio received mostly favorable reviews when it appeared and set a standard by which Cheever's later stories have often been judged. William Peden in his book on the American short story since 1940 calls it "unquestionably one of the major collections of the period." He identifies the special impact of the stories in these terms: "Beneath the often placid, impeccably drawn surfaces of his stories there is a reservoir of excitement or unrest that is capable of erupting into violence; his well-mannered characters walk a tightrope that at any minute may break; the vast, shining city masks cruelty, injustice, and evil."[8] This explains the effect of stories like "The Enormous Radio," in which the pleasant exterior of a marriage is stripped away, or "The Cure," in which a man who faces a divorce with seeming equanimity suddenly finds himself in a suicidal despair precipitated by random external events. In many of these stories the characters start from a sense of well-being only to have the order of their lives shattered by the sudden intervention of mysterious events over which they have no control; afterwards, they are never again quite as they were. The only area of critical complaint has had to do with the very well-made-ness of some of the stories. Paul Pickrel, in a predominantly favorable review, said: "If one has any criticism of this volume it is that the stories are too uniformly excellent, and of the same kind of excellence — the writing highly finished, the emotions carefully weighted and cunningly deployed, the point carefully made without calling attention to itself."[9] Pickrel and a few other reviewers expressed concern that Cheever might have been developing, through his great mastery of style, into a writer who was more flash than fire, a danger that several of them connect with his association with the *New Yorker*. However, most critics, now and in retrospect, have been impressed with the successful combination of moral thrust and storytelling skill that emerges in this volume and that will continue to dominate Cheever's writing in his first novel, *The Wapshot Chronicle*.

CHAPTER 3

"The Continuousness of Things": The Wapshot Novels

B ECAUSE John Cheever was established as a short-story writer before the publication of his first novel and since he has continued to publish in both forms, there is inevitably critical debate about his comparative skill and success in the two genres. The relatively episodic structure of his first novel, *The Wapshot Chronicle* (1957), and the fact that within its loose framework a number of diverse elements and modes work together in an uneasy amalgam have provoked some critics to assert that Cheever is essentially a short-story writer whose novels tend to be nothing more than loosely strung together episodes that would have been better realized in the form of individual stories. Nevertheless, *The Wapshot Chronicle* was quite well received by critics and honored with the 1957 National Book Award for fiction. It was also a popular success; along with its sequel, *The Wapshot Scandal,* it was Cheever's best-selling work until the publication of *Falconer.* However, critical comment on the novel tends to emphasize its charm and comic power rather than its thematic persuasiveness or its technical achievement. I suspect that finally for many readers the experience of this novel is to feel entertained, especially by some memorable characters and incidents, but a little unsure as to where they have been and to what purpose.

One reviewer judged that the characters in *The Wapshot Chronicle* "appeared to greater advantage in the short stories that were excerpted from the novel and published in *The New Yorker* than they do in the novel itself,"[1] and he attributes this difference to Cheever's tendency to let each character, as he or she appears, have center stage, forcing the others into the wings. It is true that in the novel one character tends to be featured at a time and that the sort of social interaction which we associate with the novel is held to a

37

minimum. Perhaps the fact that some of the materials of the novel did take shape for Cheever first as short stories does partly explain the sense of many readers that the elements of *The Wapshot Chronicle* never quite coalesce. Since we know that the author cast about between the short-story and the novel forms to find the most suitable expression for the Wapshot saga, it would be helpful to have some sense of what Cheever sees as the important distinctions between the two forms. But in interviews Cheever consistently begs off from theoretical explorations and, although he has commented briefly on his work in both forms, he has said very little about the short story and the novel as comparative forms. Beyond revealing that he completes a story in a matter of days while his novels have taken an average of three or four years, his only direct statement about his sense of the two forms as options for himself came in an interview shortly after the publication of the *Chronicle*. Asked if he now intended to work only in the longer form, he replied:

I'm still interested in the short story form. Certain situations lend themselves only to the short story. But generally it's a better form for young writers, who are more intense, whose perceptions are more fragmentary. A face glimpsed in a train is a short story for a young writer. As you get a little older, you lose some of this intensity, your perceptions become more protracted, and you think about the longer form.[2]

From these remarks, one can see that Cheever identifies the fragment or the isolated incident as the stuff of the short story. The complaint that *The Wapshot Chronicle* consists too much of incidents that remain isolated from an overall pattern may derive from Cheever's not having distinguished for himself, at the time of its writing, an adequate sense of how the novel might develop in contrast to the story.

Another possible explanation for the feeling that the novel doesn't ever quite pull together into a unified whole may lie in the fact that there is a strong element of autobiography in *The Wapshot Chronicle,* and the strength of Cheever's feelings about some of the autobiographical materials may at times undermine his efforts to transform them artistically. This is not to say that the novel is in any simple way based on Cheever's life and family; the resemblance between the Wapshot family and Cheever's own is ascertainable, but the two are in no way directly parallel. The closest tie exists between the Wapshots' fictional ancestor, Ezekiel

Wapshot, and Cheever's own ancestor, Ezekiel Cheever, some details of whose life as an early colonist and a Puritan are assigned to the Wapshot character. Cheever has also drawn upon his seafaring ancestors to populate the Wapshot family tree, and he seems to base some of the Wapshot family's relatives on his own cousins.

The degree to which the four members of the immediate Wapshot family are based on Cheever's own family circumstances is harder to sort out. Leander's various occupations do not connect directly with those of Cheever's father; the closest parallel is that Leander has been a businessman, as Cheever's father was. More likely, it is Leander's temperament that is related to Cheever's perceptions of his own father; he is depicted as having a zest for life, a pride in appearances, despair when his wife preempts him as family breadwinner. However, as the novel proceeds, Leander takes on almost legendary proportions, and this mythologizing complicates our sense of the autobiographical basis of his character. Leander's wife, Sarah, like Cheever's mother, derives an ecstatic satisfaction from running a gift shop and, like her, dedicates quantities of time and energy to civic responsibilities. Moses and Coverly, the sons, may be based to some extent on Frederick and Cheever himself, but Cheever has never talked in enough detail about his brother to allow us to know what the connection between character and source may be in this case. Cheever may have written his own sense of being a younger son and brother into the character of Coverly, but again he has given Coverly few characteristics or experiences that allow us easily to identify him with what we know of the author. Therefore, while *The Wapshot Chronicle* clearly makes use of autobiographical materials, we must appreciate the degree to which it is also an act of artistic invention. Yet the transformation of materials from his own life may not always have proceeded smoothly, so that it could have led to the lack of a unified impact in the novel.

One area in which invention clearly outweighs autobiography is Cheever's handling of setting. St. Botolphs, the Wapshot's home town, is a charming seaside village; Cheever himself grew up in Quincy, Massachusetts, which was even in his youth essentially a working-class suburb. The creation of St. Botolphs may owe something to the recollections of Cheever's father of Newburyport, a seacoast town where he had lived, and also to Cheever's own observation of New England villages. But St. Botolphs is most significantly an imaginative creation, like Twain's St. Petersburg, Ander-

son's Winesburg, and Faulkner's Jefferson. The credibility with
which he depicts St. Botolphs led one reviewer of a later novel to
register a complaint that greatly amused the author, who recounted
it in an interview:

It said that I missed greatness by having left St. Botolphs. Had I stayed, as
Faulkner did in Oxford, I would have probably been as great as Faulkner.
But I made the mistake of leaving this place, which, of course, never
existed at all. It was so odd to be told to go back to a place that was a complete fiction.[3]

In St. Botolphs Cheever has created an ideal setting which would
allow him to explore certain themes and values and which would
stand in contrast to the more realistic locales, including Washington, D.C. and New York City, to which some of his characters will
move.

The novel is divided into four parts. Part One is a straightforward, chronological narrative of the Wapshot family's lives from a
Fourth of July celebration with which the novel opens to the end of
the summer and the departure of the sons from home to seek their
fortunes at the demand of Honora, their father's cousin and holder
of the family pursestrings, who has decided they are old enough to
set forth to see if they can earn the legacy she proposes if they make
their ways in the world. Part Two alternates in an irregular pattern
chapters of Leander's journal or autobiography, begun when the
boys leave home, with chapters about their adventures in the cities
to which they go. Part Three continues with the experiences of
Moses and Coverly; these experiences involve primarily their
attempts to find wives and to father heirs so as to meet the requirements of Honora's legacy. Except for the dropping of Leander's
journal, this section is mostly a continuation of the previous one.
Its separate standing may be justified by the fact that the boys' particular quest of matrimony and fatherhood is crucial if they are to
receive their inheritance, and thus it may deserve a special focus.
Part Four has only two short chapters, one recounting Leander's
death and funeral, the other involving a brief trip home by Coverly
with his family on another Fourth of July. The novel ends almost
abruptly. Some sense of structural unity is provided by the fact that
the novel begins and ends with the celebration of the Fourth of
July, but in the light of the novel's loose structure, this coming full
circle seems a little forced. It may be justified thematically by the

novel's concern with ceremony and celebration, but it tends to be disconcertingly tidy in the light of the novel's looseness of form.

The novel's title may illuminate to some extent Cheever's handling of form; certainly part of the novel's point is to chronicle the Wapshot family, immediate members and ancestors. Consequently, the use of revealing episodes that capture the essence of the characters, as well as the inclusion of the autobiographical journal of Leander, may be necessary and justified. But one must ask why the Wapshots are deserving of a chronicle, or what point is made of their lives. This is the hardest question to answer about the novel: whether or not it adds up to more than an entertaining gallery of portraits of characters who have a series of comic and poignant adventures. I think that it does. The chronicling of characters and adventures finally contributes to an overriding thematic concern — the issue of whether or not one can make the traditions of the past usable in a present which increasingly devalues tradition altogether. A continuing thread of concern with a usable past emerges through the adventures of the main characters and their reactions to them.

The most fully developed characters in *The Wapshot Chronicle* are Leander and his cousin, Honora Wapshot, who possesses the family fortune and uses it to try to influence the others. At first, Leander and Honora seem to be opposites, representing perhaps the two major directions taken by the New England cultural/religious heritage. Honora seems to represent the spiritual side, with its tendency to make narrow judgments on life and behavior; Leander stands more for the sensuous side, with its ability to accommodate and assimilate all manner of experience. Neither character functions, however, in a simple or allegorical fashion. Honora's moral sternness is complicated by a real love of nature and a spontaneous capacity to enjoy certain pleasures, such as movies or Boston Red Sox games, although she hypes their pleasurability by sneaking off to them as though they were illicit. At the same time, the predominance in Leander's character of a responsiveness to the sensuous side of life is balanced by a respect for tradition and ceremony and a desire to pass on to his sons usable and substantial values. How mixed is his outlook on the world is made clear in a letter he leaves for his sons to read after his death:

"Advice to my sons," it read. "Never put whisky into hot water bottle crossing borders of dry states or countries. Rubber will spoil taste. . . . Bathe in cold water every morning. Painful but exhilarating. Also reduces horniness. Have haircut once a week. Wear dark clothes after 6 p.m. Eat fresh fish for breakfast when available. Avoid kneeling in unheated stone churches. Ecclesiastical dampness causes prematurely gray hair. Fear tastes like a rusty knife and do not let her into your house. Courage tastes of blood. Stand up straight. Admire the world. Relish the love of a gentle woman. Trust in the Lord." (pp. 306–07)[4]

This mixture of superstition, concern for good manners, and genuine moral guidance informs Leander's life and behavior throughout the novel.

In the course of the book, Honora and Leander do occasionally function as adversaries; certain episodes emphasize their real differences. For instance, although she was herself married briefly to a European count of dubious title, Honora seems almost punitively virginal, like Dickens's Miss Havisham. Because she discovered Moses with a girl, she decided to force him to leave home and seek his fortune, and she stops at nothing to get his parents to acquiesce in her plan (It may not be sexuality *per se* but its expression outside the rituals of marriage that she is reacting against). Leander, on the other hand, speaks consistently in the novel for sensuous experience, fully apprehended, and consequently he is the dominant counter-influence to the strictures of Honora's moral norms. However, although Honora more often speaks for spiritual values, narrowly held, and Leander for earthly pleasures, vigorously enjoyed, they finally are shown to be able to participate at least partially in each other's values. The earthy Leander, for instance, refuses to tell his sons the facts of life because:

It was his feeling that love, death, and fornication extracted from the rich green soup of life were no better than half-truths, and his course of instruction was general. He would like them to grasp that the unobserved ceremoniousness of his life was a gesture or sacrament toward the excellence and the continuousness of things. (p. 53)

Although their form and direction may be different, Leander can appreciate the need for governing ritual and ceremony, as Honora can. And Honora's behavior at Leander's funeral reveals her similar flexibility. Despite her wish to have everything the way it always has been for the Wapshots — the Gospel of John rather than Corinthians, as she reminds the minister in mid-service — and warned by the minister of the impropriety, she nevertheless insists at Leander's graveside that Coverly recite, as was Leander's wish, the closing lines of *The Tempest:* "We are such stuff as dreams are made on, / And our little life is rounded with a sleep."

Leander and Honora are the titanic figures of *The Wapshot Chronicle,* representing in their vitality and even in their eccentricity the power of the tradition of which they are so conscious of being descendants. Honora cites exemplary experiences and inspiring quotations from Wapshot ancestors; Leander composes a journal so as to take his place in the grand lineage of Wapshots, inveterate diarists, and underline in his life "the continuousness of things." These two characters, energized by their sense of the past and determined to convey, in their own individual ways, the power and usefulness of tradition to the next generation, are the most fully realized characters in the novel and the most important in raising it from a simple photograph album, as one critic called it, to a novel with a thematic point.

One of the oddities of characterization in the novel involves the role of Sarah Wapshot, Leander's wife. Her role as mother of the boys would seem to make her potentially as important in the novel as Leander is, but she is markedly less developed a character than either Leander or Honora, and she plays an unpredictably limited part in the novel's events. This treatment of her may reflect Cheever's ambivalence about his own mother, upon whom Sarah is based to some degree. (Cheever revealed that one consideration in publishing this novel was to delay it until after his mother's death.) Also, since the novel involves the struggle of Honora and Leander to lead fulfilling lives and to influence the direction of the boys' lives, Sarah gets lost in the shuffle. Nevertheless, although as much space is devoted to her as to Honora — though not so much as to Leander, whose journal dominates Part Two — she doesn't have much effect at crucial moments in the novel like the boys' departure from home or Leander's funeral. It is left to her to ride on the Woman's Club float in the Fourth of July parade, to coo over a young woman she takes in after an auto accident, and to turn Leander's beloved ferryboat, the *Topaze,* into The Only Floating Gift Shoppe in New England. Her influence on the boys, her power to affect her husband other than by preempting his livelihood, and even her connection to the New England heritage that dominates the lives of Leander and Honora, except perhaps for her civic-mindedness reminiscent of the nineteenth-century social reformers, are very tenuous. Of the major characters in *The Wapshot Chronicle* she is the least memorable and the least thematically important.

Whereas Leander and Honora are the most important characters in the novel in terms of their values, Moses and Coverly are most important in terms of the plot development of the novel. It is their participation in the archetypal experience of young men leaving home and childhood to make their ways in the adult world that serves as the main story line of *The Wapshot Chronicle*. The boys are not developed in much psychological depth; more emphasis is placed on their experiences than on their reflection upon their experiences. It may be this treatment of Moses and Coverly, as much as anything, that has led some critics to regard the book as essentially an entertaining comic-picaresque tale. Their adventures are indeed treated in the way we would expect in the picaresque mode. What happens to them is most often a result of chance or accident; the more serious events that befall them do not have long-lasting effects but are often countered by fortuitous good luck; and some of their experiences, such as the battery of psychological tests Coverly undergoes in order to get a job in a carpet factory, are obviously intended as social criticism of the world through which the boys move.

Moses goes first to Washington, D.C., where through a connection of Honora's he gets a job in a top-secret agency. He loses the job as easily as he got it; his security clearance is lifted when he is denounced by a woman with whom he has had a brief affair. In a Hemingway-style move, he goes fishing to think things over; in a Horatio Alger twist, he rescues the mistress of a wealthy New York businessman, who promptly takes a shine to Moses, sends him to bond school, and gives him a high-paying job in his New York firm. Meanwhile, Coverly, in New York, having failed the psychological tests that would have qualified him to work in the carpet factory, works on a loading dock and at night goes to school to learn to be a computer taper. He graduates and immediately gets a job with the federal government, which unceremoniously ships him off to an isolated missile base in the South Pacific, an exile which is terminated when he manages to get home after receiving a telegram saying that Leander is dying, only to discover that Leander sent the telegram himself because he is lonesome.

Except that it indicates that they can support themselves, the boys' finding jobs is not terribly important in the novel, except as a vehicle for some mild social satire. More important is their search for wives, and here a difference between Moses and Coverly begins to emerge. Coverly's quest is short and unexciting. He is a domestic, uxorious man; and soon after he arrives in New York, he meets Betsy, a waitress whose most distinguishing trait is an almost pathological loneliness. He moves in with her, marries her, and would live happily ever after if she did not leave him periodically during attacks of depression. She does, however, return to him with just as little explanation as attends the boys' finding jobs; and at the end of the novel, Coverly's domestic happiness, marked by the birth of a son, seems relatively assured.

Moses has a more exciting romantic quest. He falls in love with Melissa, the ward of a wealthy old woman, Justina Wapshot, a distant relative of the St. Botolphs clan. Justina, who lives in a preposterous castle assembled from various rooms imported from foreign chateaux and cathedrals, is a man-hater and places Moses's room as far from Melissa's as possible. To get to her, he climbs naked over the roofs and turrets each night. Whereas Coverly's search for a wife was simple and conventional, Moses — a satyr where Coverly is a husband — engages in a comic-chivalric trial in an inauthentic medieval setting to outwit the witch and win the damsel. He is successful, and by the end of the novel he too is married and the father of a son. Since the boys have met the requirements of Honora's will, the legacy is distributed, and Moses and Coverly are on their way to St. Botolphs to buy Leander a new boat with some of the money when he dies.

The handling of Leander's death helps us see the technique of characterization which Cheever is employing in *The Wapshot Chronicle*. Put simply, the major characters, especially Leander, are portrayed realistically and at the same time invested with mythic stature. For instance, Moses and Coverly are simultaneously ordinary young men involved with work and women and archetypes of the initiate entering the world of adult experience. Justina is both a rude, dictatorial old woman and a witch or dragon to be outsmarted by the hero. Leander, on one hand a father, husband, cousin, citizen of St. Botolphs, and descendant of an old New England family, is also a mythic figure, most like a sea-god. Cheever makes use of mythic analogues throughout his fiction, pointing out in one interview that "the easiest way to parse the world is through mythology."[5] But he tends for the most part to avoid the use that John Updike made in *The Centaur* of specific gods and mythological tales as sources; rather he uses archetypal situations or general mythic parallels in a manner more resonant than literal. A small exception to this general rule occurs in *The*

Wapshot Chronicle at a moment in which Leander feels estranged from Coverly and there is a reference to Icarus — "as if the boy had fallen away from his heart" (p. 60); but such direct references are rare. The treatment of Leander's death is an example of how Cheever usually invokes myth. One Sunday morning Leander astonishes St. Botolphs by attending church; the following morning he goes to the beach.

> He waded out to his knees and wetted his wrists and forehead to prepare his circulation for the shock of cold water and thus avoid a heart attack. At a distance he seemed to be crossing himself. Then he began to swim — a sidestroke with his face half in the water, throwing his right arm up like the spar of a windmill — and he was never seen again. (p. 302).

Whether or not Leander intended suicide is left ambiguous. The unusual attendance at church and the apparent crossing of himself as he enters the water point in the direction of a deliberate death, but the precautionary splash of water to avoid a heart attack works in the other direction. Most important are the literary and mythic analogues — a reminder of Prospero and *The Tempest* in death by water, an echo of Don Quixote in the reference to the windmill spar, and, most important, a mysterious death and an unrecovered body. As Frederick Bracher observes, "Like a god or culture hero, his disappearance from earth is mysterious and ceremonious."[6] But lest we be left too simply with a sense of Leander as purely legendary, the description of his funeral places him firmly again within a daily pattern of life in society. The church is so crowded that Honora, upon entering, blurts out, "Who are all these people?"

> They were the butcher, the baker, the boy who sold him newspapers and the driver of the Travertine bus. Bentley and Spinet were there, the librarian, the fire chief, the fish warden, the waitress from Grimes' bakery, the ticket seller from the movie theater in Travertine, the man who ran the merry-go-round in Nangasakit, the postmaster, the milkman, the stationmaster, and the old man who filed saws and the one who repaired clocks. (p. 304)

Yet even this catalogue, while emphasizing the capaciousness of Leander's workaday life and interests, also leaves us feeling, once again, that he was larger than life. Thus Cheever's method of characterization plays back and forth between the realistic detail and the legendary impact. The purpose of this mythologizing in

The Wapshot Chronicle seems to be to invest the past, the traditions which have informed the life of Leander, and the crucial events of his sons' initiation into adulthood with extra meaning. It is as though in a world which has less and less appreciation for tradition, tradition itself needs to be augmented with legendary and mysterious qualities so as to win our consideration. The more mysterious, the more mythic Leander seems to be, the more difficult his sons will find it to ignore the meaning of his life and his world.

This quality of the novel connects to one theme which does emerge in it and even provides a degree of unity among the diverse elements. I have already mentioned a difference between Moses and Coverly, whose quest for adulthood provides the momentum of the novel; in their pursuit of women Moses is more sensual, Coverly more domestic. But there is a more significant contrast between them, which is prefigured early in the novel. Leander takes his sons in turn on a ritual fishing trip when each is old enough. Moses loves the experience and takes to it naturally; but when Coverly's turn comes, he has a cold, is uncertain about wanting to go, and obediently brings along a book his mother has slipped him: *500 Ways to Prepare Fish.* Leander is infuriated by the inappropriateness of this behavior, and Coverly wonders about his status as son to his father. But from this unpromising contrast between the boys, the novel develops in a surprising direction. Coverly, perhaps *because* of the reflectiveness growing out of his feelings of separation or distance from his father, becomes more of a real son to his father. He is the one who returns when the fake telegram arrives. Despite being the younger son, he is the one who pronounces the final words over his father's grave. To the extent that the novel has a governing theme, it resides in the goal Coverly sets himself: "To create or build some kind of bridge between Leander's world and that world where he sought his fortune..." (p. 118). Moses is almost like Leander incarnate and only the sensuous side of Leander at that. Coverly, differing more greatly from his father, seems to have a better vantage point really to see and appreciate the older man's life and values; and he consciously sets out to assimilate the traditional values and find a way to use them in his own life. Thus, it is thematically appropriate that the novel ends with Coverly returning with his family to participate once again in the continuing ritual observance of the Fourth of July in St. Botolphs.

And it seems to me that this thematic concern with the question of usable tradition and how it can be passed on in an increasingly untraditional world at least partly justifies the form which Cheever has used in this novel. Since Leander is the character who is most consciously aware of trying to pass on a sense of tradition and ceremony to his sons, both the episodes which reveal his own use of tradition and the chapters from his journal are important to the development of the theme. And since Coverly is the character who is consciously trying to receive and retain the sense of tradition and ceremony which his father wishes to impart to his sons, the use of the archetypal situation of the young man leaving home to make his way in an alien world also seems indicated. *The Wapshot Chronicle* is not a tightly structured, "well-made" novel, by any means, but some of what Cheever has chosen by way of form for his novel is, I think, understandable in the light of his concern for the issue of a usable past. Finally, the difference which he establishes between Moses and Coverly, with its thematic implications is going to become even more crucial in the continuation of their story in *The Wapshot Scandal*.

I   The Wapshot Scandal *(1964)*

For all that it is a continuation of the saga of the Wapshot family of St. Botolphs, *The Wapshot Scandal* is a very different kind of novel from *The Wapshot Chronicle*. Separated from its predecessor by the publication of two volumes of short stories, it represents for the author a considerable shift in both outlook and technique, including a looser structure than that of the *Chronicle,* an increased focus on American culture and social problems, and, consequently, significantly decreased attention to the Wapshots themselves. Coverly is clearly the central character of the novel; Honora is important but treated more as an eccentric than as the repository of family tradition; and Moses is less and less important, although his wife, Melissa, seems to be, after Coverly, the novel's most important character. *The Wapshot Scandal* is a very difficult novel to get a grip on. If one is expecting a simple sequel to *The Wapshot Chronicle,* disappointment is the most likely reaction. Social criticism of cultural phenomena of the early 1960s sometimes seems to be the main issue, but it is undercut by the idiosyncratic nature of the characters, especially Coverly, who is the observer of much of what is passed on to us. Whether Coverly, with his bucolic back-

ground, is a meaningful observer of the contemporary scene is a question. Is the clash of his values with those around him to be read as a critical comment on those of his world or as a comic discontinuity? The novel isn't absolutely clear on this important point; consequently, it is hard to be certain whether we are reading about the modern world's tragic falling away from St. Botolphs and the values it represents or about a comic juxtaposition of the norms of the new world with those of the old.

Cheever himself indicates that writing *The Wapshot Scandal* was a difficult experience. Admitting to a sense of "clinical fatigue" after finishing any book, he gave one interviewer this account of his feelings which indicates that his worst postpartum experience was with *The Wapshot Scandal:*

> I'd never much liked the book and when it was done I was in a bad way. I wanted to burn the book. I'd wake up in the night and I would hear Hemingway's voice — I'd never actually heard Hemingway's voice but it was conspicuously his — saying, "This is the small agony. The great agony comes later." I'd get up and sit on the edge of the bathtub and chainsmoke until three or four in the morning.[7]

Furthermore, to the degree that the Wapshots and St. Botolphs, however worked over by the author's imagination, are still partly the autobiographical residue of Cheever's problem-ridden youth, the whole matter may resist his efforts to give it form and pattern. There is some reason to wonder whether the writing of *The Wapshot Scandal,* with its killing off of the last pillar of the past and the apparently final departure of the sons, isn't at least partly an act of exorcism. Following as this novel does the publication of Cheever's most curious volume of short stories, *Some People, Places, and Things That Will Not Appear in my Next Novel* — in which some critics have professed to see a conscious plan to depart in the future from certain themes and techniques — *The Wapshot Scandal,* too, may be seen, as Eugene Chesnick suggests, as a departure from St. Botolphs and what it meant to Cheever's sense of the past — America's and perhaps his own.[8] But, has Cheever, in his attempt to recreate and imaginatively handle this aspect of his past, found that it can be carried along into the contemporary world in some assimilated, adapted form, or must it finally be buried, revered as a relic but judged essentially irrelevant to the world of the 1960s? The experience of Coverly in the novel, presiding at the end over

Honora's customary Christmas dinner, seems to lead him to be able to integrate the two worlds with some success, but the experience of Moses, Melissa, and Honora herself suggests the opposite conclusion.

The question of autobiography in this novel is very hard to ignore, especially when one considers Cheever's disposition of the character of Sarah Wapshot, mother of the boys. As we noted, she is given a surprisingly insignificant role in *The Wapshot Chornicle,* although the reasons for her lack of prominence and impact on the lives of her husband and sons in that novel are really not clear. In *The Wapshot Scandal,* written after his own mother's death, Cheever expresses the nature and motivations of the character of Sarah very negatively, and the terms of the complaint echo things Cheever has said about his own mother. At the time of the novel, both Leander and Sarah are dead, but while Leander continues to be a presence in this novel — even appearing in ghostly form to Coverly — Sarah is dismissed in these bitter sentences, only barely relieved by a tone of irony:

Mrs. Wapshot died two years later and ascended into heaven, where she must have been kept very busy since she was a member of that first genera- tion of American women to enjoy sexual equality. She had exhausted her- self in good works. She had founded the Woman's Club, the Current Events Club, and was a director of the Animal Rescue League and the Lambert Home for Unwed Mothers. As a result of all these activities the house on River Street was always filled with dust, its cut flowers long dead, the clocks stopped. Sarah Wapshot was one of those women whose grasp of vital matters had forced them to consider the simple tasks of a house to be in some way perverted. (p. 19)[9]

All of this comes close to the picture Cheever has developed in interviews of his mother, herself founder of a Current Events Club, businesswoman and activist rather than homemaker, and often not accessible to her family. The important point here, however, is that the apparent directness of this literary portrait of Cheever's mother underlines the fact that the St. Botolphs world is, to some degree, an autobiographical matter, a complex rendering of a complicated relationship between the author and his past. In this novel, more than in its predecessor, the focus seems to be on the cultural values of that past rather than on the nature of its particular human relationships.

Consequently, characterization in *The Wapshot Scandal* seems

proportionately less important a fictional element than it was in *The Wapshot Chronicle.* This may be due in part to the greater emphasis in the later novel on the direct depiction of social phenomena and problems; as Cynthia Ozick says, "...The chief character is the 20th century...."[10] Social issues do play an unprecedentedly large role in the novel's dynamics, and their prominence tends to push the characters into the background or forces them into the constricted terms of their societal dilemmas and defeats. Also, efforts to discuss the characters tend to end up in accounts of what each one *does.* This may be a function of what Glenway Wescott calls Cheever's "existentialist" mode: "He reveals his people by what happens to them, and by what they happen to be doing at a given moment, and what they remember having done, rather than by exact analysis on his part or important articulateness of their own."[11] This emphasis on social issues and active modes of characterization may also account for the huge number of characters who appear in this novel — by Wescott's count, half a dozen Wapshots, at least that many other principal characters, twenty-five characters who figure in some of the episodes involving the principals, and perhaps fifty more minor characters who appear briefly.

Most surprising to the reader of the first Wapshot novel, however, are certain omissions and changes of emphasis in characterization. In addition to the absence of Leander and Sarah (both dead), Moses figures surprisingly little in the novel. Already fading into the background by the end of the *Chronicle,* he has practically no role in this novel other than to fall apart and become a drunkard when he learns of his wife's infidelity. Melissa, on the other hand, important only as the girl Moses sought to marry in the first novel, is central in *The Wapshot Scandal;* the midlife crisis which overtakes her is treated with dignity and compassion. Honora is less important in this novel than in the former; she appears much less frequently, and when she does, her eccentricity is emphasized more than her power. Coverly has moved fully stage center and dominates the novel as much as any single character. But, as in the previous novel, the degree of interaction between characters is very limited; each lives out his or her own drama almost privately. Coverly has several encounters with Moses and is with Honora when she dies, but never sees Melissa in the course of the novel. Honora and Melissa, both exiles in Rome at one point in the novel, never meet. Except for the meaning which Coverly tries to draw from the life of Honora, as from his father's earlier, these characters live and suffer separately, and the non-Wapshot characters are even more tangentially related to any sense of a whole pattern.

The ascendancy of Melissa to a central role in this novel throws light on Cheever's intention in *The Wapshot Scandal*. While in the *Chronicle* she functioned entirely as the desirable damsel of Moses's quest, in the *Scandal* she becomes a character of major interest, in the process overshadowing Moses. She is important in this novel mainly for her experience of a cruel midlife crisis which begins with boredom, is exacerbated by a serious illness, leads to marital infidelity, and ends with exile. Although the terms in which Melissa's crisis takes place may strike the reader of the 1970s as very limited in its presentation of a woman's situation, nevertheless, Cheever's awareness of women's dissatisfaction and restlessness precedes the real flowering of the women's movement and is an early version of a heroine besieged by an identity crisis. Although, as Wescott pointed out, most characters in this novel are not permitted deep reflection or eloquent articulateness, the major characters are given these qualities to some degree. Part of our sympathy for Melissa may derive from the fact that we are allowed to know some of her thoughts and feelings throughout her trials. Also, as often happens in Cheever's work, a random juxtaposition of events in her life conspires to break through the defenses against chaos which she has built in her suburban world: an afternoon visit in which she is told by an ill-intentioned gossip of a neighbor, Gertrude Lockhart's, infidelity with the grocery delivery boy is followed by a typical party in Proxmire Manor at which she finds herself bored early in the evening. She reflects: "Loneliness was one thing..., but boredom was something else, and why, in this most prosperous and equitable world, should everyone seem so bored and disappointed?" (p. 50). Going in search of the bathroom, she mistakenly enters a darkened bedroom, only to find that she has interrupted the tryst of two housewives, an event so extraordinary that she concludes that the women must be from outside Proxmire Manor. Vaguely stirred by the story of Gertrude Lockhart and the scene in the bedroom, Melissa returns to the party feeling

...a profound nostalgia, a longing for some emotional island or peninsula that she had not even discerned in her dreams.... Its elevating possibilities of emotional richness and freedom stirred her. It was the stupendous feeling that one could do much better than this ... that the world was not divided into rigid parliaments of good and evil but was ruled by the absolute authority and range of her desire. (pp. 50–51)

The marriage of Moses and Melissa is based almost entirely on their sexual compatibility, and they turn out to have nothing else in common; and from this moment of insight at the party, Melissa goes in search of some greater fulfillment. She is impelled in this by a serious bout with pneumonia which makes her aware of the fleetingness of life; her quest is also catalyzed when she learns of Gertrude Lockhart's suicide. However, her circumstances offer her nothing more fulfilling than Emile, the teenaged delivery boy from the grocery store. She has an affair with him which is discovered by his mother, who tells Moses; he leaves her and spends the rest of the novel drinking. Melissa goes to Rome with her son after Emile places on her lawn a promotional Easter Egg containing a free trip. At the end of the novel, Emile is reunited with Melissa in Italy, and they embark on further sensual adventures. Yet the fact that we are not meant to write Melissa off as an inconstant wife or a lust-driven woman is supported by her attempts throughout the story to regain her equilibrium. However, nothing in her life provides a chance for meaningful stability. She goes to her minister, but he interrupts her confession of infidelity to recommend a psychiatrist. And in our final view of Melissa in the novel Cheever does his best to invest her situation with almost tragic dignity as she shops in a supermarket:

Grieving, bewildered by the blows life has dealt her, this is some solace, this is the path she takes.... Tears make the light in her eyes, a glassy light, but the market is crowded and she is not the first nor the last woman in the history of the place to buy her groceries with wet cheeks.... No willow grows aslant this stream of men and women and yet it is Ophelia that she most resembles, gathering her fantastic garland not of crowflowers, nettles, and long purples, but of salt, pepper, Bab-o, Kleenex, frozen codfish balls, lamb patties, hamburger, bread, butter, dressing, an American comic book for her son and for herself a bunch of carnations ... and when her coronet or fantastic garland seems completed she pays her bill and carries her trophies away, no less dignified a figure of grief than any other. (p. 298)

But, of course, Chever would not need to make that last assertion if he didn't realize that there is a problem here, that the investing of the domestic routine of Melissa and the form of her crisis with tragic significance is going to require a sympathetic, imaginative leap by the reader. This passage really delineates the nature of the tragedy as much as the tone Cheever means to assume in regard to it; the scene underlines again that there are inadequate options for a woman in American culture. Neither domestic routines nor sordid affairs are sufficient to the need Melissa felt for a more fulfilling life. Melissa is the brightest, most vital and sensitive woman yet created by Cheever; hence, the consequences of a world which does not allow her avenues to identity and outlets for her awareness are treated by Cheever as, in fact, tragic.

Honora is, of course, one of Cheever's most memorable women characters, but she has the luxury of being the patriarch (no one would accuse her of being matriarchal) of the clan, the holder of the pursestrings, and also the possessor of a sense of identity which comes easily if one is a member of one of the oldest families in a small town. But in this novel she is treated with less seriousness than in *The Wapshot Chronicle;* and in the light of her actual behavior in the *Scandal,* Coverly must work overtime to invest her life with meaning just as Cheever had to in regard to the mundane and almost sordid circumstances of Melissa's. For one thing, Honora plays a surprisingly small role in *The Wapshot Scandal;* she appears in only four of its thirty-two chapters and is mentioned anecdotally in two others. Furthermore, she is treated here as particularly eccentric. When her crisis strikes, she exhibits some strength of character; but we see nothing like the established set of values associated with her in the *Chronicle.* Also, she does commit suicide in this novel — and the handling of the event is far less ambiguous than Leander's death in *The Wapshot Chronicle;* it is as though she declares herself irrelevant or inadequate to the world of the mid-twentieth century.

Honora's crisis involves the government's discovery that she has never paid an income tax. In *The Wapshot Chronicle* this fact was generally known by the family but treated as one of her many idiosyncracies, like not paying bus fares and sending the bus company a check once a year. In this novel, as the twentieth century impinges more and more on the world of St. Botolphs, an IRS man shows up on her doorstep to declare that she is a criminal and will be indicted. Her lawyer, old Judge Beasely, advises her to withdraw money from the bank and flee to Europe rather than risk the poor farm. Honora buys a length of clothesline and goes to the attic to hang herself; in the midst of this she comes upon Leander's journal and begins to read. The text begins: "Cousin Honora Wapshot is a skin flint'' and goes on to charge that she refuses to lend money to her only cousin while performing numerous charities throughout the town (pp. 82–83). Leander then goes on to recount some of his amorous adventures. Somehow, the effect of this is to dissuade Honora from her planned suicide because the next we see of her she is on a ship bound for Europe. In a hilarious but not very well integrated chapter, published first as ''The Traveller'' in the *New Yorker* (December 9, 1961), we see Honora's sense of rootlessness as the boat sails, followed by her fury at some fellow travelers who recount their last European trip entirely in terms of the kind of clothes-drying weather they found in each city for their orlon wardrobes and capped by her befriending a con man who has stowed away on the ship. She also manages to blow out the ship's generators twice by plugging in her old-fashioned curling iron, one of the few triumphs in the novel of her way of life over the contemporary world. Once she is in Europe, we see virtually nothing of her except for a comic audience with the Pope in which neither understands a word the other says, a fact which doesn't bother the Pope since he has understood her to say, in answer to a question about her home, that she is from San Bartolomeo, and he chats about the beauty of that town. The next time we see her is the day the IRS man shows up at her hotel with an extradition order. Relieved, ready to return home, she draws her money out of the bank, and on the way to the airport distributes it to everyone she meets. She leaves Italy with the recipients of her final largesse kneeling in the streets blessing her. She then returns to St. Botolphs and starves herself to death before the trial date. Coverly arrives in time to sit at her side, keep her bourbon glass replenished, and read aloud to her from *The Count of Monte Cristo,* as they had done together in his childhood. Coverly's grief is mitigated by her sense that she is going to her death on her own terms. Honora extracts from Coverly a promise that he will return at Christmas to preside over her annual Christmas dinner to which she has already invited twelve strangers as she does every year. As Coverly, more and more her true heir just as he was increasingly his father's truer son, watches over her final hours, he reflects:

...that she would not, after all, ever die. She would stop breathing and be buried in the family lot but the greenness of her image, in his memory, would not change and she would be among them always in their decisions. She would, long after she was dust, move freely through his dreams, she would punish his and his brother's wickedness with guilt, reward their good works with lightness of heart, pass judgment on their friends and lovers even while her headstone bloomed with moss.... The goodness and evil in the old woman were imperishable. (p. 296)

Clearly, this is a personal act of imaginative assimilation by Coverly; it becomes clear that for Moses no such sense of personal continuity with the past and its values sustains him.

As already indicated, Coverly is the brother who is central in this novel; Moses appears seldom and when he does, he is clearly bankrupt both financially (he has borrowed improvidently against Honora's legacy, which must now go to pay back taxes) and emotionally. Upon learning of Melissa's infidelity, he starts drinking and is never sober again in the novel. It is left to Coverly alone to try to complete the task he set himself in the earlier novel: to build a bridge between Leander's (and Honora's) world and the one in which he lives. The degree of difficulty in such a task is made clearer in this novel than in its predecessor as Cheever takes us more deeply into the problems of the mid-twentieth century. The problem is indicated by a detail of setting: the missile base where Coverly works adjoins an abandoned farm, too irrelevant even to be worth the trouble to raze the buildings. Coverly, because he is the one with an appreciation for the past, has the most sensitivity to aspects of the present most inimical to the values of his upbringing. Early in the novel, he returns to the empty family home and is visited by Leander's ghost. His response, "Oh, Father, Father, why have you come back?" echoes through the rest of the novel at times of particular stress.

One way in which Coverly tries to build his bridge between the two words is to attempt to turn technology to humanistic ends, programming a computer to discover the incidence of certain words in Keats's poetry, but no one finds the results interesting. Coverly tries to take seriously the speeches at a conference he attends, but instead the real clash between his outlook on life and the contemporary world becomes clear to him:

The legal vocabulary was familiar but Coverly couldn't grasp its applicability to the cosmos. He could not easily apply phrases like National Sovereignty to the moon. The following lecture dealt with experiments in sending a man into space in a sack filled with fluid.... Coverly wanted to approach the scene with his seriousness — with a complete absence of humor — but how could he square the image of a man in a sack with the small New England village where he had been raised and his character had been formed? ... Leaving the lecture hall, he ran into Brunner and asked him to lunch. His motive was curiosity. Compared to Brunner's high-minded scientific probity the rhythms of his own nature seemed wayward and sentimental. Brunner's composure challenged his own discipline and his own usefulness and he wondered if his pleasure in the unscientific landscape of the Atlantic City boardwalk was obsolete. (pp. 178–79)

Coverly is the one, early in the novel, who realizes that we are all "ransomed to our beginnings" (p. 67), but the fact that to remain in touch with the positive part of one's past is an act of will is made clear by Coverly's behavior in the novel. Only he returns to see his family home and to sit at Honora's death bed. Only he, of the men at work at the missile site, has enough distance to wonder about what they are doing and its implications for the future and to worry about what guidance to give his son in this rapidly changing world. And, at the end of the novel, he returns — despite his wife's feeling that it is unnecessary and ridiculous to honor the wish of Honora — to host her planned dinner at Christmas.

The contrast between Coverly and Moses, which began to develop in *The Wapshot Chronicle,* becomes absolutely clear in this novel. The narrator in Chapter Two briefly introduces the Wapshot family for those who aren't familiar with the earlier novel; he delineates the brothers clearly:

Moses ... had the kind of good looks and presence that sweeps a young man triumphantly through secondary school and disappointingly enough not much farther. ... Everybody loved Moses, including the village dogs, and he comported himself with the purest, the most impulsive humility. Everybody did not love Coverly. He had a long neck and a disagreeable habit of cracking his knuckles. (p. 19)

This misleadingly slight mention of Coverly is counteracted by our discovery that it is his life and awareness that will dominate the book; he figures in eleven chapters to Moses's four. Later, the narrator again calls our attention to the differences between the two boys:

What had happened, what had happened to Moses Wapshot? He was the better-looking, the brighter, the more natural of the two men and yet in his early thirties he had aged as if the crises of his time had been much harsher on a simple and impetuous nature like his than on Coverly, who had that long neck, that disgusting habit of cracking his knuckles and who suffered seizures of melancholy and petulance. (p. 243)

Again Cheever provides no real clue as to *why* Coverly is surviving the 1960s better than Moses; it is hard to believe that it has to do with his long neck and his knuckle-cracking. We know relatively little about his temperament and his motivations and in fact witness very little of the petulance and melancholy the narrator mentions. From the previous novel and from Coverly's behavior in this one, we are left to surmise that it is his reflectiveness, his attempt to retain some connection with the past, and his greater family orientation that distinguish him from his brother. At the end of the novel, we see Moses in total collapse. On Christmas Eve, he is discovered in a hotel room in St. Botolphs, inebriated and in the company of a town prostitute. Coverly, who has attended the midnight service at the Episcopal church to observe the holiday, goes to bring him home. The next morning, Moses, with a mighty hangover, thinks: "The brilliance of light, the birth of Christ, all seemed to him like some fatuous shell game invented to dupe a fool like his brother while he saw straight through to the nothingness of things" (p. 303). Coverly meanwhile courteously hosts the Christmas dinner to which Honora had this year — with a devastating irony in view of most of the characters' blindness to the passing away of traditions — invited patients from the Hutchins Institute for the Blind. There is no doubt that Cheever feels that Coverly has, despite his occasional wrenching perceptions of the discontinuities between past and present, the better lot.

As one considers what has happened to the major characters, one wonders exactly what Cheever intended by his title. Is the scandal in question Honora's imminent disgrace as a tax cheat? Melissa's infidelity? Moses's collapse? Community reaction to Honora's situation is never shown, and her sense of disgrace is all interior; public scandal never materializes. Melissa's behavior is suggested as symptomatic of the times more than as scandalous; it provokes a complete marital rupture because of Moses's pride rather than because of social disapprobation. Moses's financial and emotional bankruptcy develops offstage, and no one's reaction to it figures in the novel. No scandal touches Coverly's life. The title seems oddly chosen, too strong a word for the events that befall the protagonists or for any public reaction to them. The book seems more an elegy, for the last of the titanic generation as it passes with Honora, for the promise of Moses, for the vitality of Melissa, for St. Botolphs itself. This elegiac tone is emphasized in the lines that conclude the novel, when the narrator says: "I will never come back, and if I do, there will be nothing left, there will be nothing left but the head-stones to record what has happened; there will really be nothing at all" (p. 307).

Like its predecessor, *The Wapshot Scandal* derives some structural unity from beginning and ending with a holiday celebration in St. Botolphs, in this case, Christmas. Chapter One of the novel recreates Christmas Eve in the village, complete with carolers, tree-trimming tableaux, and midnight Mass at the Episcopal church, but punctuated by discordant notes such as a tearful phone call to faraway relatives from the drugstore pay phone and the accidental drowning of a lonely old man who was trying to do away with a pillow case full of unwanted kittens. The final chapter depicts Honora's traditional Christmas dinner. But except for this unifying device, *The Wapshot Scandal* is even more random in its structure than *The Wapshot Chronicle*. It seems to pursue a relatively straightforward chronological line of development, focusing in turn on Coverly, Melissa (with some reference to Moses), and Honora, but the stage is usually occupied by just one character at a time with such minimal interaction between the main characters that the movement back and forth between them is jerky and gives us a "meanwhile, back at the ranch" feeling. Also, the novel jumps around erratically between settings other than those where the main characters live, and it focuses in considerable detail on minor characters such as the IRS man or Cameron, the head of the missile site and Coverly's boss. Both of these characters have whole chapters devoted to them; yet little is done to connect them to the Wapshots and so provide at least some unity for the history.

A further problem of unified effect derives from Cheever's handling of point of view. It seems to be omniscient. Most of the book is told from the third-person point of view, but in some places a narrator becomes very direct and personal and uses first person pronouns. All of Chapter Two, for instance, is devoted to the narrator's personal recollections of the Wapshots, and he reveals the emotional investment he as author/narrator has made in the chronicling of their lives in an earlier volume. The last lines of the novel also involve the *narrator's* plan to leave St. Botolphs, with no reference to the Wapshots. However, it isn't clear exactly who this narrator is (though he seems to have an authorial connection to the material); his presence is not constant; and his deeply personal interventions amid long stretches of objective third-person narrative make for a jerky effect in the novel's telling.

Although *The Wapshot Scandal* contains sections of writing that are as good as anything Cheever had done to date, some of the sections tend to be isolated set-pieces, hilarious or poignant, but finally not contributing to an identifiable, overall design. And, because structure guides our responses, the looseness of this novel is likely to make the reader feel that, despite the vividness of certain scenes and the velocity of the telling, we really do not quite know what the novel is driving toward.

Although this novel may be Cheever's loosest, least carefully plotted, he himself has remarked on his attitude toward narrative in a way that may be illuminating:

I don't work with plots. I work with intuition, apprehension, dreams, concepts. Characters and events come simultaneously to me. Plot implies narrative and a lot of crap. It is a calculated attempt to hold the reader's interest at the sacrifice of moral conviction. Of course, one doesn't want to be boring ... one needs an element of suspense. But a good narrative is a rudimentary structure, rather like a kidney.[12]

Perhaps the vigor of his language here owes something to the fact that he has been criticized for a relative lack of attention to narrative structure, in the novel form at least. His later novels appear to display more concern with architectonics. Nevertheless, plot itself as well as the dynamic development of character does get short shrift in his novels, and the reason may lie in the preference he declares for intuition, apprehensions, dreams, and concepts. Or, as he said in the same interview when asked if fiction should give moral lessons, "No, fiction is meant to illuminate, to explode, to refresh."[13] *The Wapshot Scandal* does those things with great effectiveness; but whether a reader can maintain the illumination and the refreshment of isolated moments without the sustaining aid of a narrative that makes comprehensive sense out of those moments is the main critical problem of the novel.

Perhaps the element which most distinguishes *The Wapshot Scandal* from its predecessor is the amount and the force of social criticism which it includes. One chapter begins: "Now that was the year when the squirrels were such a pest and everybody worried about cancer and homosexuality" (p. 94). Not only does this line remind us of American concerns in the early 1960s, but the juxtaposition of the squirrels with the other grounds for anxiety indicates Cheever's sense of the trivializing of feeling which may be the worst danger in a world in which change is the only constant. Coverly functions in the novel as one observer of the changes space-age technology is bringing about, and his inability to completely bridge his new world and the world of St. Botolphs is finally a comment on the contemporary scene. Another forum in which the same point is made is a Senate subcommittee before which Cameron, head of the missile site, testifies. An elderly senator, after listening to the testimony, breaks down in tears and pleads:

"We possess Promethean powers but don't we lack the awe, the humility, that primitive man brought to the sacred fire? . . . If I should have to make some final statement. . . , it would be in the nature of thanksgiving for stouthearted friends, lovely women, blue skies, the bread and wine of life. Please don't destroy the earth, Dr. Cameron," he sobbed. "Oh, please, please, don't destroy the earth." (p. 215)

Mawkish and oversimplified as the senator's response to Cameron is, it also serves in context as an antidote to the excessively scientific discourse that has been going on, taking no account of human values. This point is underlined when, later in the hearing, Cameron, the supertechnocrat of the novel, is revealed to have punished his young son so cruelly years before that he has been institutionalized for most of his life. The novel also deals with life in the suburbs and its enforcing of social conformity, bored housewives, airplane hijacking, alcoholism, government bureaucracy, and attitudes toward death, to name only some of its targets for social criticism. Much more than its predecessor, it has the feeling of its time period. Cheever has said in an interview that while in his stories he strives for universality of experience, he believes at the same time — this in the context of talking about Fitzgerald's work — that "all great men are scrupulously true to their times."[14] Of all of Cheever's fiction, this novel is the closest in settings, social phenomena, and details of everyday life to the times in which it was written.

Consequently, we have in this novel a mixed bag — a sequel to *The Wapshot Chronicle,* a polemic novel of social criticism, a book with comic episodes but an overridingly autumnal mood. Critical response has been very mixed. Those who like it use words like "inventive" and "delightful"; those less enthusiastic mention its structural problems and the question of its sentimentality. Several critics suggest that in moving the novel away from St. Botolphs, except for Coverly's three visits, Cheever is trying to deal with

American society as a whole. However, this may be exactly the
source of what some feel is the weakness of the novel; perhaps it
needed to be either more completely a sequel to the earlier Wapshot
novel or more completely separate from the world of St. Botolphs.
Cynthia Ozick suggests that the novel is an uneasy mixture and
hence ineffective social criticism:

Now it is on this myth of St. Botolphs that Cheever as social critic finally
crashes.... Nobody can inherit it because nobody had a grandfather who
lived there, and to take St. Botolphs as a touchstone of a living society is to
raise a tombstone to any possibility of satirizing that society.[15]

The juxtaposition of the mellowly lit St. Botolphs world with the
world of missile sites and suburbs makes St. Botolphs seem more
eccentric, more like a sort of Never-Never-Land, than it did in *The
Wapshot Chronicle,* where the same contrast did not develop so
fully; and as Ozick says, since the town lacks the feel of substantial-
ity, it does not provide an adequate standpoint from which to criti-
cize the real world of the early 1960s. It seems to me that another
problem is that we are led by the titles to expect a degree of continuity between the Wapshot novels that is not forthcoming. The
lesser seriousness of Honora in the *Scandal* is disconcerting, the
number of characters in the novel with little or no connection to the
Wapshots pulls us away from a sense of sequence, and the presence
of a narrator who was not present in the *Chronicle* is further confusing. It seems that probably what is really happening between the
covers of *The Wapshot Scandal* is an attempt on the part of
Cheever to make some sort of personal peace with the past, with
family memories, with the place and time of his upbringing, while
as an author, his attention is being drawn more and more to the
social problems and cultural phenomena of his immediate times.
The result is, in some places, confusing; in other places, brilliant. It
will remain for *Bullet Park,* Cheever's next novel, to demonstrate
that he can unify novelistic materials in an effective manner.

CHAPTER 4

Love and Usefulness: Life in
Shady Hill and Elsewhere

SOME of the finest American short stories of the twentieth century appear in two of Cheever's story collections, *The House-breaker of Shady Hill* (1958) and *Some People, Places, and Things That Will Not Appear in My Next Novel* (1961). Both volumes contain stories that are among Cheever's very best work, and some of the stories have been so frequently anthologized that they are undoubtedly his best-known fiction. These two volumes were published between *The Wapshot Chronicle* and *The Wapshot Scandal*, and careful analysis of Cheever's achievement in these stories will help us understand some of the shifts in focus and theme which we have noted between the first Wapshot novel and its sequel. Such analysis will also indicate what a fine craftsman can do with the form of the short story.

George Garrett has suggested that these two volumes are "...so constructed as to qualify as novels if the definition of that form is at last liberated from certain arbitrary restrictions."[1] Probably most serious readers of fiction have liberated the definition of the novel enough to see Hemingway's *In Our Time* and Anderson's *Winesburg, Ohio,* as novels despite the fact that their "chapters" have the separate integrity of short stories. Most readers would have little difficulty seeing Cheever's *The Housebreaker of Shady Hill* as novelistic in the sense that *Winesburg* is. All the stories take place in the suburb of Shady Hill, and there is some interaction between various minor characters. While there is no George Willard figure to act as confidant, catalyst, and unifying device, one could also say that his role is taken by Shady Hill itself, a location which functions very much like a character in these stories. It would be much more difficult, however, to justify *People, Places, and Things* as a novel despite what seems to be some effort on the author's part to give the collection some coherence. It has no unity of setting, nor does point of view, theme, or tone connect the stories to each other in a convincing way. The most important thing about both collections, after all, is not whether they are novelistic in conception or design but that they show Cheever really hitting his artistic stride in the short-story form.

I   The Housebreaker of Shady Hill and Other Stories (1958)

This volume may be Cheever's most uniformly excellent collection of short stories. Except for two stories, "The Sorrows of Gin" and "The Trouble of Marcie Flint," these stories are not only successful but nearly flawless. The problem in the two exceptions I've named seems to lie primarily with point of view. "The Sorrows of Gin" starts out from a twelve-year-old child's point of view and tries to deal with her perception of the place of alcohol in her parents' life. Amy observes her parents' and their neighbors' drunken behavior and is encouraged by a housekeeper to pour out her father's gin now and then if she cares for him, only to discover that the housekeeper is herself a lush and then inadvertently to provoke a fight between her babysitter and her father over a bottle Amy has emptied. The story ends with Amy trying to run away from home and with a sudden reverie, from her father's point of view, about the mysteriousness of children and the sweetness of home. The pieces of the story never add up to a dramatic whole. The other story that doesn't quite coalesce, "The Trouble of Marcie Flint," begins with a journal being kept on board ship by a man, Charlie Flint, who is leaving his wife because of her infidelity. Her lapse, however, seems to have been precipitated by his own mysterious three-month absence from home. It ends with his plan to return to his wife as soon as the ship docks, but just why he has changed his mind isn't clear. The story is dominated rhetorically by Charlie's journal, but the dramatic focus is on the plight of Marcie, trying to fill the emptiness in her life with activities, including a Shady Hill planning board battle over whether or not a library is a civic improvement which will attract undesirable new residents. She has an affair with her only ally in the battle, but its motivation is nearly as unclear as that of her husband's absence and planned return. The story leaves a dominant impression of the superficiality and enforced conformity of the suburban way of life that is, however, complicated and even contradicted by some of the other stories in this collection.

Alfred Kazin explains the essential nature of the Cheever story of this period as follows:

The subject of Cheever's stories is regularly a situation that betrays the basic "unreality" of some character's life. It is a trying-out of freedom in the shape of the extreme, the unmentionable. Crossing the social line is one aspect of comedy, and Cheever demonstrates it by giving a social shape to the most insubstantial and private longings. Loneliness is the dirty little secret, a personal drive so urgent and confusing that it comes out a vice. But the pathetic escapade never lasts very long. . . .

In these terms the short story becomes not the compression of an actual defeat but the anecdote of a temporary crisis.[2]

This description fits many of the stories in *The Housebreaker of Shady Hill.* Though the circumstances which propel the characters into their "temporary crises" vary — from Johnny Hake's loss of his job in "The Housebreaker of Shady Hill" to Francis Weed's escape from death in an airplane crash in "The Country Husband" to Will Pym's jealousy about his wife's coming home late from a party in "Just Tell Me Who It Was" to her husband's extended absence in "The Trouble of Marcie Flint" — for the most part their tryings-out of some form of freedom or expression are deliberately eschewed or thwarted by external factors and the characters reintegrated into their social milieu despite its problems or drawbacks. Only in "O Youth and Beauty!" is the hero destroyed altogether; only in "The Five-Forty-Eight" is a Shady Hill protagonist a participant in a crisis initiated by an outsider. Finally, "The Worm in the Apple," a *tour de force* on the subject of happiness and contentment, stands completely apart from these other stories and counteracts some of the concerns that they express.

In the title story, "The Housebreaker of Shady Hill," Johnny Hake suddenly loses his job through the machinations of corporate infighting. In the only first-person narrative in the collection, Johnny expresses his pleasure in the comfortable suburban life he has been leading:

We have a nice house with a garden and a place outside for cooking meat, and on summer nights, sitting there with the kids and looking into the front of Christina's dress as she bends over to salt the steaks, or just gazing at the lights in Heaven, I am as thrilled as I am thrilled by more hardy and dangerous pursuits. . . . (p. 3)[3]

But Shady Hill is expensive; and with bills mounting, Johnny Hake sneaks into the unlocked home of one of his wealthy neighbors and steals $900 from his wallet. Immediately, he feels cut off from the society which means so much to him that he has become a thief in order to remain in it. In a development typical of Hawthorne, he suddenly begins to see signs of dishonesty all around him: a businessman pocketing a waitress's tip, a man selling phony uranium stocks, the newspapers full of robberies. He becomes preternaturally sensitive; when a friend tries to throw him an easy piece of brokerage business, referring to it as a "steal" and a "burglary," Johnny becomes physically ill. When his children give him an extension ladder for his birthday, he panics and imagines that he has been talking in his sleep about his new role as a second-story man. On his way to his second burglary, it begins to rain and his career as a criminal is suddenly at an end. He says:

> I wish I could say that a kindly lion had set me straight, or an innocent child, or the strains of distant music from some church, but it was no more than the rain on my head ... that showed me the extent of my freedom.... I was not trapped. I was here on earth because I chose to be. (pp. 28–29)

And just as suddenly as Johnny's return to the moral framework of his society is effected, so is he suddenly — with almost as little explanation — restored to his job. Getting an advance on his salary, he replaces the stolen money, and all is again right with the world. The story is very like a fable. The fortuitous events and changes of heart would be irritating if it weren't clear that the point of the story is finally the importance of being in phase with the moral order of one's world.

In "The Country Husband," perhaps the best story in the collection and winner of an O. Henry award, the separation of the protagonist, Francis Weed, from his society is also initiated by an outside force. He is on an airplane which crash-lands safely. Thanks to the miracles of modern travel, he manages to get back to New York in time to catch his usual commuter train to Shady Hill; and in this familiar setting, he can hardly believe in his narrow brush with death, much less convey it to the neighbor sitting next to him. He walks into his house hoping for a sympathetic audience, but his children are squabbling and his wife preoccupied with dinner, and he has no one to help him respond to this extraordinary moment. A few nights later another event breaks the routine of Francis's life. At a party, he identifies the maid serving canapes as a French woman whom he had seen being punished for collaboration with the Germans during World War II. But at the same moment that he recognizes her, he realizes that he can tell no one, for in his circumstances:

...it would have been a social as well as a human error. The people in the Farquarson's living room seemed united in their tacit claim that there had been no past, no war — that there was not danger or trouble in the world. In the recorded history of human arrangements, this extraordinary meeting would have fallen into place, but the atmosphere of Shady Hill made the memory unseemly and impolite. (p. 59)

Once again, Francis is left alone with an important moment in his life; the effect on him is to leave him "...feeling languid; it had opened his memory and his senses and left them dilated" (p. 59). At this vulnerable moment, Anne Murchison, the babysitter, steps into the light on the porch, and Francis falls in love. The brief emotional fling which follows reveals Francis's need for a fuller emotional life and results in a rebellion against the constrictions of his society. He dreams of running off with Anne; and in the grip of this heady emotion, he insults the reigning grande dame of Shady Hill society, an incident comic in its telling but important also for provoking Francis to a recognition of his current social demeanor:

Among his friends and neighbors, there were brilliant and gifted people ... but many of them, also, were bores and fools, and he had made the mistake of listening to them all with equal attention. He had confused a lack of discrimination with Christian love, and the confusion seemed general and destructive. (p. 65)

His feeling for Anne has been beneficial, he believes, giving him a zest for life as well as increasing his critical judgment. However, his feeling also leads him into an act which separates him morally from the community. Out of jealousy at learning that Anne, with whom he has only a fantasy relationship, is engaged, he tries to ruin her fiance's chances for a job in the city. Overcome with guilt, he decides to see a psychiatrist, the same Dr. Herzog who keeps reappearing in Cheever's fiction. After his tearful declaration, "Dr. Herzog, I'm in love," we see nothing more of their session, but we learn at the end of the story that Francis has taken up wood-

working as a hobby. More important, he has been willingly reab-
sorbed into the community. In a catalogue of his neighbors and
their nightly activities, Francis appears unostentatiously in the middle, building a coffee table in his cellar. In Kazin's terms, he may
have gotten a glimpse of his alienation, but he has also learned that
there are no viable alternatives. The story ends with the image of
Jupiter, the dog that undermines all order in Shady Hill; only ani-
mals are allowed to indulge their anarchic impulses, and even they
will not get away with it forever.

"Just Tell Me Who It Was" is a much slighter story than either
of these, but it is, nevertheless, effectively developed. It involves
Will Pym, who has married a much younger wife, whom he dotes
upon and, in the course of the story, comes unfairly to suspect of
infidelity. His suspicion stems from her appearance when she
comes home late from a country-club ball: her costume has been
torn in the dancing, she has lost her pocketbook, and — feeling
jaded and disillusioned in the early morning — she enters the house
crying. Will awakes, sees the torn costume and her tears, and
assumes she's been with another man. He reassures her that it
doesn't matter to him. The seed of distrust planted, however, he
becomes obsessed by the question of her fidelity, remembering
every lateness with doubt, searching through her closet for some
sort of clue, snapping at friends in whose innocent joking he now
hears sexual innuendoes. Finally, he decides "who it was," walks
up to the imagined culprit on the commuter train platform, and hits
him. After this violent act, he feels restored and plans to buy Maria
some expensive jewelry as a sign of his forgiveness, "something no
young man could afford" (p. 162). Despite the fact that his suffering has been self-induced, Will too now feels reintegrated into his
marriage and happy way of life. Unless his wife takes offense at
being forgiven for a sin which she did not commit, this couple may
return to their former tranquillity, although one wonders if Will
can ever again be totally free of this sort of suspicion.

Along with "The Country Husband," the other masterpiece of
this volume is "O Youth and Beauty!," the only story in the collection n
which the protagonist is completely destroyed. It is impossible not to see
the similarity between this story and Hemingway's "The Short Happy
Life of Francis Macomber," since both end with wives shooting their
husbands. In Cheever's story, however, the hero's movement is negative, a deterioration, rather than a positive development like Macomber's finding his courage and manhood. Cash Bentley, a forty-year-old

businessman who was a college track star, can be depended on, at the end of most Shady Hill parties, to move the furniture around into a simulated hurdles course. Someone fires a gun, and he's off. "There was not a piece of furniture in Shady Hill that Cash could not take in his stride" (p. 34). One night, however, Cash falls and breaks a leg, and this catastrophe precipitates in him dark presentiments of gloom and death, just as his act of robbery caused Johnny Hake to see corruption everywhere. Suddenly Cash is overwhelmingly aware of the smell of rotting meat in the refrigerator, the touch of a spider web in the attic, the ugliness of an elderly prostitute in the city, the rank odor of earth on the autumnal roses his wife brings in from the garden. He notices how his acquaintances all seem to be aging, and he is rude and irritable to everyone with whom he talks. Watching some young people dance at a party next door, he is overcome with jealousy:

> He does not understand what separates him from these children in the garden. He has been a young man. He has been a hero. He has been adored and happy and full of animal spirits, and now he stands in a dark kitchen, deprived of his athletic prowess, his impetuousness, his good looks — of everything that means anything to him. He feels as if the figures in the next yard are the specters from some party in that past where all his tastes and desires lie, and from which he has been cruelly removed. (p. 43)

Although everyone undergoes some sense of trauma at the sense of aging, Cash's problem is exacerbated by the suddenness with which the crisis is thrust upon him and also, as the above passage indicates, by the absence of any other competence or satisfaction that he values in his life. He is another character like Tom Buchanan in *The Great Gatsby,* but he doesn't miss the playing fields of his youth as desperately until this crisis, perhaps because he has been able to recreate at least some of the glory in his party performances. After his convalescence, some friends persuade him to come to the country club; at the end of the evening, he runs the hurdles again, clearing all the furniture but collapsing winded and sick at the end of the course. The next night, bored at the weekend's dwindling away, he arranges the furniture in his own living room and calls his wife to come down and fire the starting pistol for him.

> He had forgotten to tell her about the safety, and when she pulled the trigger nothing happened.

"It's that little lever," he said. "Press that little lever." Then, in his impatience, he hurdled the sofa anyhow.

The pistol went off and Louise got him in mid-air. She shot him dead. (p. 46)

Hemingway makes it comparatively clear that Margot Macomber shot her husband deliberately; here Louise's behavior is finally ambiguous. There is evidence that Cash has been cruel to his wife during his convalescence as well as some suggestions about how heavily the family's precarious financial state falls on Louise, forcing her into grueling economies and late-night chores. If there is anything involved in the shooting, however, other than the purest accident, it seems most likely to be an almost humane desire to put a wounded animal out of its misery, for Cash surely is like a racehorse who will never again be able to run. Even though he successfully clears the furniture in his last run at the club, the exhaustion it costs him makes clear that his career as a perpetual youth is over. The story ends with an ambiguous act; yet one cannot help but feel that, given the limitations of his outlook on life, Cash probably is better off dead. He is unlikely to be able to adjust gracefully to the realities of aging and death.

"The Five-Forty-Eight," which won the Benjamin Franklin award, differs significantly from the other stories in this collection in that the Shady Hill protagonist is a totally unlikable character with whom we are not intended to sympathize. Cheever's intent here is signaled by his giving the character only a last name, Blake; furthermore, although a wife is mentioned, Cheever gives us no details of children, house, station wagon, or other humanizing data about Blake's life. The story involves an act of vengeance against the man undertaken by a woman he has misused. She was his secretary; he slept with her, then had her fired to avoid complications. Unfortunately for Blake, the woman has a history of mental illness; and after being unable to get in to see him in his office, she follows him to his train, the five-forty-eight to Shady Hill. When he tries to move away, she shows him a gun in her purse. He wishes one of his neighbors on the train would notice his plight, but it is revealed that he has quarreled with the only ones in his car — Mrs. Compton, because she sympathized with Blake's wife after he mistreated her, and Mr. Watkins, for being an artist and free spirit and hence a bad influence in the community — and they understandably ignore him. He is left alone at the station with a madwoman, who apparently wants no more violent revenge than to force him to kneel down in the street and put his face in the dirt. He does so, weeping, and she turns and walks away. The last line of the story, "He got to his feet and picked up his hat from the ground where it had fallen and walked home" (p. 134), in its flat matter-of-factness leaves us believing that no rude awakening into an enlarged humanity has taken place for Blake. The only effect that thinking he is going to die has on him is to make him notice more vividly the homes, the lights, the street signs of Shady Hill, perhaps as symbols of the security which is now in doubt for him; his reflections are marked by no thoughts of family and no regret or guilt about his treatment of the woman. This story is an odd addition to the volume; it adds no real insight into Shady Hill as a community, and it provides the only unrelievedly despicable character from Shady Hill in the book. It is very well paced dramatically, and it achieves its degree of horror by the placement of ominous events in the familiar setting of other stories in the volume. Fictionally, it is a good story, but thematically it is rather out of phase with the rest of the Shady Hill stories.

"The Worm in the Apple" is a funny little *tour-de-force* with an underlying serious point. It is more a sketch than a story; it deals with the Crutchmans, who were "...so very, very happy and so temperate in all their habits and so pleased with everything that came their way that one was bound to suspect a worm in their rosy apple and that the extraordinary rosiness of the fruit was only meant to conceal the gravity and the depth of the infection" (p. 107). The story consists of little more than the narrator's pointing out some apparently happy aspect of the Crutchmans' lives and then expressing the community's skepticism about it. Why do they have so many picture windows in their home? "Who but someone suffering from a guilt complex would want so much light to pour into their rooms?" (p. 107). Every single favorable aspect of their lives is attributed to some inner weakness — Helen's attractive pallor to possible nymphomania, Larry's gardening without a shirt to infantile exhibitionism. Yet, the narrator has to admit, things *seem* to be all right. Helen has inherited a fortune, but her husband still goes to work every day instead of becoming a drunken wastrel, and they give money to charity and live modestly. Nor does any unhappiness emerge in the children, though the community trains its scrutinizing eye on them for some clue of family dishevelment. In the course of their social lives, the more promiscuous members of the community have made overtures to both Larry and Helen but have been consistently put off. "What was the source of this constancy? Were they frightened? Were they prudish? Were they monogamous? What was at the bottom of this appearance of happiness?" (p. 109). Their children grown and happily married, the Crutchmans proceed to age gracefully, and the story tells us that they "got richer and richer and richer and lived happily, happily, happily, happily" (p. 112). By now the point is probably clear. As in James's *The Sacred Fount*, the reader is drawn at first into a hunt for secret sin or sorrow in the lives of these characters, only to realize that perhaps there is none, that perhaps things, in this case, *are* what they seem, and that to seek for a worm in the apple is a reflection on those who never doubt the appearance of defeat or depravity but who are much slower to believe in happiness and uncomplicated pleasure in life. The story functions in the collection as an antidote to what could be the reader's tendency after reading the stories of Johnny Hake, Francis Weed, and Cash Bentley to suspect that all the homes in the suburb of Shady Hill conceal some deep sadness or debilitating moral weakness and thus to miss the point of some of those same stories — that the moral balance can be restored, that a meaningful life can be lived, in the suburbs as well as anywhere else.

All but two of these stories use an omniscient narrator; Johnny Hake narrates his own story in "The Housebreaker of Shady Hill," and "The Sorrows of Gin" seems to switch from omniscient to limited third-person point of view within the story. The intrusions of the narrator are not so obvious in all the stories as in "The Worm in The Apple"; however, we are never unaware of a narrative presence. The use of this fictional device will increase in the next volume of short stories, *People, Places, and Things;* and, as I have already mentioned, Cheever will use, intermittently, a full-fledged author/narrator in *The Wapshot Scandal*. The high degree of authorial presence, along with the handling of setting and the placement of evocative details or anecdotes, is one of the most distinguishing characteristics of Cheever's fiction, one which we see developing in this volume and continuing in the books which follow. George Garrett has observed that some of the freedom which Cheever has introduced into the short-story form comes from his "...much more positive exploitation of the narrator-writer of the story. He appears openly like the chorus of an early Elizabethan play, does his best to establish an intimacy and rapport with his reader, and then cheerfully re-enters from time to time to point out significant objects or to make an intelligent comment." Garrett goes on to suggest that the purpose of this technique of Cheever's is that: "It wants to *say more,* not only about persons, places and things, but about what these things mean, what patterns they make."[4] Cheever resembles Fitzgerald much more than Hemingway in this handling of point of view, being willing to intervene, being likely to express a lyrical vision in terms of his own outlook rather than fitting it to the perspective of a character within the story. When he wants to write a taut, suspenseful story with no authorial intervention, he can — as he does in "The Five-Forty-Eight"; but the general feeling of most of Cheever's memorable stories owes a great deal to his willingness to be the presiding genius of the world which he depicts.

Another element which comes through most strongly in the stories in *The Housebreaker of Shady Hill* is setting, but one immediately notices how few trees, ponds, winding roads, and gently sloping hills contribute to one's sense that one *knows* Shady Hill. For Cheever, again like Fitzgerald rather than Hemingway, setting is more a matter of artifacts and is created heavily by accounts of manners. A description of the living room of Francis Weed's Dutch Colonial home will suffice to show how Cheever uses things themselves and human behavior to create a sense of place:

The living room was spacious and divided like Gaul into three parts. Around an ell to the left as one entered from the vestibule was the long table, laid for six, with candles and a bowl of fruit in the center.... The largest part of the living room centered around a fireplace. On the right were some bookshelves and a piano. The room was polished and tranquil, and from the windows that opened to the west there was some late-summer sunlight, brilliant and as clear as water. Nothing here was neglected; nothing had not been burnished. It was not the kind of household where, after prying open a stuck cigarette box, you would find an old shirt button and a tarnished nickel. The hearth was swept, the roses on the piano were reflected in the polish of the broad top, and there was an album of Schubert waltzes on the rack. (pp. 51–52)

Cheever doesn't always give us the interiors of his characters' houses in such detail. In this case, his purpose is served; the conventionality of the life that goes on in the house, evoked by the obligatory bowl of fruit as a centerpiece, and especially the almost sterilized good housekeeping of Julia Weed, is underlined. Another of

Cheever's devices for establishing a strong sense of the Shady Hill setting is to catalogue the behavior of its inhabitants as he does, for instance, in the opening lines of "O Youth and Beauty!":

At the tag end of nearly every long, large Saturday-night party in the suburb of Shady Hill, when almost everybody who was going to play golf or tennis in the morning had gone home hours ago and the ten or twelve people remaining seemed powerless to bring the evening to an end although the gin and whiskey were running low, and here and there a woman who was sitting out her husband would have begun to drink milk; when everybody had lost track of time, and the baby sitters who were waiting at home for these diehards would have long since stretched out on the sofa and fallen into a deep sleep...; when the bellicose drunk, the crapshooter, the pianist, and the woman faced with the expiration of her hopes had all expressed themselves; when every proposal — to go to the Farquarsons' for breakfast, to go swimming, to go and wake up the Townsends, to go here and go there — died as soon as it was made, then Trace Bearden would begin to chide Cash Bentley about his age and thinning hair. (p. 33)

Cheever also excels at the evocative incident which captures some aspect of the nature or quality of either a place or of his characters' lives. These are often well-written little segments that function so completely in and of themselves that they run the danger of straining the fabric of the story. An excellent example is the description of a little girl, Gertrude Flannery, in "The Country Husband":

Gertrude was a stray. She had been born with a taste for exploration, and she did not have it in her to center her life with her affectionate parents.... Garrulous, skinny, and unwashed, she drifted from house to house around the Blenhollow neighborhood.... Opening your front door in the morning, you would find Gertrude sitting on your stoop. Going into the bathroom to shave, you would find Gertrude using the toilet. Looking into your son's crib, you would find it empty, and looking further, you would find that Gertrude had pushed him in his baby carriage into the next village. She was helpful, pervasive, honest, hungry, and loyal. She never went home of her own choice. When the time to go arrived, she was indifferent to all its signs. "Go home, Gertrude," people could be heard saying in one house or another, night after night. "Go home, Gertrude." "It's time for you to go home now, Gertrude." ... "Go home, Gertrude, go home." (p. 67–68)

Such little sketches, amusing as this one is in creating the image of a chorus saying "Go home, Gertrude" rising throughout the neighborhood, have practically no function in the story except that

Francis will try to kiss the babysitter in his vestibule only to discover Gertrude standing there. In the light of that minimal function, the above passage seems almost out of proportion; it does, however, convey a sort of fact of existence in neighborhoods, most of which have some sort of Gertrude figure, and in this way the segment contributes to the reader's overall sense of place.

Cheever's attitude toward suburbia in these stories is mixed. The most negative story on this score is "The Trouble of Marcie Flint," wherein Charlie Flint begins with a catalogue of all the things he will not miss about life in the suburbs:

"God preserve me ... from women who dress like *toreros* to go to the supermarket, and from cowhide dispatch cases, and from flannels and gabardines. Preserve me from word games and adulterers, from basset hounds and swimming pools and frozen canapes and Bloody Marys and smugness and syringa bushes and P.-T.A. meetings." (p. 165)

Charlie, however, is fleeing a marital disappointment and cannot be read as reliably objective. More critical in this story is the situation in which people on the planning board vote against building a library on the grounds that it will attract undesirable new residents to Shady Hill. In the rest of the stories, however, life in Shady Hill is shown to be pleasant and relatively innocent; gentle images such as that of a family having their Christmas card picture taken in front of their house in August abound. However, Shady Hill is also a world in which money is crucial to happiness and where social conformity can be enforced. Cheever does note the awfulness of Sunday afternoons after weekends of too much drinking, the tendency of the community to erase any part of the past that is painful or inconvenient, and an excessive concern for propriety on the part of many residents. But it is also a world in which much that has gone awry can be reconciled at the Communion rail — to which many Shady Hill residents repair in varying degrees of piety — or in the marriage bed or in a touch football game. There is a sense in this way of life of strenuousness contained within patterns of the characters' own choosing. One will have to wait for stories and novels yet to come for a more severe criticism of life in suburbia.

This volume does show, however, some interest in the role of women in this society, an issue that points forward to the situations of Melissa Wapshot and Gertrude Lockhart in *The Wapshot Scandal.* Although the protagonists in most of these stories are men, their wives are given some in-depth attention. The portrayal of Johnny Hake's wife in "The Housebreaker of Shady Hill" is typical, but perhaps most thorough. One of her typical days is recounted by her husband:

Drive me to the train. Have the skis repaired. Book a tennis court. Buy the wine and groceries for the monthly dinner of the Societe Gastronomique du Westchester Nord. Look up some definitions in Larousse. Attend a League of Women Voters symposium on sewers. Go to a full-dress lunch for Bobsie Neil's aunt. Weed the garden. Iron a uniform for the part-time maid. Type two and a half pages of her paper on the early novels of Henry James. Empty the wastebaskets. Help Tabitha prepare the children's supper. Give Ronnie some batting practice. Put her hair in pin curls. Get the cook. Meet the train. Bathe. Dress. Greet her guests in French at half past seven. Say *bon soir* at eleven. Lie in my arms until twelve. Eureka! You might say that she is prideful, but I think that she is a woman enjoying herself in a country that is prosperous and young. (p. 20)

This description of an excess of energy and variety of activities does not appear to be intended as a satiric portrait; Christina Hake comes across in the story as capable of doing and enjoying all these things. Louise Bentley, on the other hand, is portrayed as suffering because of the family's financial worries. We are told that "...her life was exacting and monotonous. In the pockets of her suits, coats, and dresses, there were little wads and scraps of paper on which was written, 'Oleomargarine, frozen spinach, kleenex, dog biscuit, hamburger, pepper, lard...' " (p. 35). She spends hard days coping with the housework and four children without the hired help most of her neighbors enjoy or the respite of activities outside the home: "Snowsuits, shoes, baths, and groceries seemed to have permeated her subconscious. Now and then she would speak in her sleep — so loudly that she woke her husband. 'I can't *afford* veal cutlets,' she said one night" (pp. 35–36). Louise is a woman without many outlets for her energies, as are some of Cheever's other women, but one nearly worn out by her responsibilities. Her exhaustion must be considered in trying to decide whether her shooting her husband is an accident or not; it is possible that she cannot conceive of taking on the care of one more child. Julia Weed, on the other hand, is closer to the stereotype of the suburban woman too involved with social considerations. She has a weakness for parties which, we are told,

...sprang from a most natural dread of chaos and loneliness. She went through her morning mail with real anxiety, looking for invitations, and she usually found some, but she was insatiable, and if she had gone out seven nights a week, it would not have cured her of a reflective look — the look of someone who hears distant music — for she would always suppose that there was a more brilliant party somewhere else. Francis limited her to two week-night parties, putting a flexible interpretation on Friday, and rode through the weekend like a dory in a gale. (p. 57)

That this amounts to an essentially critical portrait of Julia is made clear when she fails to respond to her husband's near-miss in the airplane crash and also when her only reaction to his increasingly aberrant behavior is to resent his rudeness to one of the arbiters of Shady Hill social life because it might mean a decrease in party invitations. All in all, the women in *The Housebreaker of Shady Hill* are not destructive or hopelessly trivial, but Cheever shows an awareness of the dangers of life for women in an affluent society if they do not have avenues to a feeling of usefulness and meaning in their lives. It is a subject he will return to again.

If there is a weakness to any of these stories, it is in Cheever's reliance on sudden, fortuitous escapes from or alleviations of his characters' difficulties. The crises in these people's lives are real and painful, but the ends of the crises come so abruptly and, in some cases, with so little plausibility, that it may be hard for the reader to feel their seriousness. Johnny Hake ends his life as a burglar because the rain begins to fall; just as suddenly, he gets his old job back. Francis Weed is saved from his crisis by woodworking. Charlie Flint plans to return to the wife he has just left for no explained reason. It never occurs to Flint that his wife may not want him back, nor to Will Pym that *his* wife may resent his forgiveness since she committed no indiscretion. Into lives wracked with real pain, real healing comes — it is even possible to see Cash Bentley's death as a healing solution to what ailed him — but this healing comes by chance or by sudden shifts of feeling that are not really explained. In his next volume of short stories as well as in the novels to come, Cheever will tend to show his characters being more deeply affected and changed by their behavior. There will be fewer miraculous escapes.

II Some People, Places, and Things That Will Not Appear in My Next Novel *(1961)*

This book, a collection of stories titled *Some People, Places, and Things that Will Not Appear in My Next Novel,* is an odd but interesting volume. It contains some very good stories, although, as a collection, it is not as even as *The Housebreaker of Shady Hill*. A number of the stories are set in locations not previously employed by Cheever, primarily Rome or other Italian settings. One story seems to involve Moses Wapshot in Proxmire Manor, but nothing about the character with his name is reminiscent of the Moses of the Wapshot novels. Another story is set in Shady Hill and seems a fugitive from that volume. The title and an unusual sort of preface have led some critics and reviewers to attempt to justify the collection as a unified whole; George Garrett felt, as has been mentioned, that it was "novelistic" in design. But I agree with Eugene Chesnick who really doesn't see such unity in the collection and makes the point that

nothing is to be gained by perversely overstating the significance of this thin volume as the turning point in a career except that Cheever himself uses the occasion to declare that he has grown impatient with many of the themes of our literature and is determined to seek out new ones.... To his immense credit he does not bog down in complaints about the inadequacy of art, but instead makes a serious attempt to define what can still be done in fiction and produces a few worthwhile stories as he does so.[5]

Cheever indicates his plan for the volume in an unconventional way, letting himself be "quoted" in a sort of preface which reads almost like jacket copy but which appears on a separate page before the title page. After an introductory sentence (by whom we do not know) we read this statement, supposedly a quotation of Cheever:

In order to become readable again, to say nothing of recouping some of its lost importance, fiction can no longer operate as a sixth-rate boarding-house. And in a world that changes more swiftly than we can perceive — where even the mountains seem to shift in the space of a night — the process of eviction, of selecting characters of stature, can be as interesting as the final cast.

The other "speaker" continues: "In a sense, then, these libelous and compassionate stories are a series of envoys to people and situations whose claim on our attention is intense but not (Mr. Cheever hopes) final." This statement of authorial intention, taken together with the title and the final piece in the volume, a sort of essay about other characters whom he wishes to evict from his future work, has led people to consider whether or not this collection adds up to a unified artistic statement. I think not, but at the same time there are some devices, settings, and concerns which emerge in this work which will be dealt with more fully in *The Wapshot Scandal,* published three years later, and in subsequent volumes of short stories as well.

The first story, "The Death of Justina," is also somewhat responsible for the reader's sense of at least an attempt at a unifying perspective in the volume, though it seems to me that a sense of such connectedness breaks down as the remainder of the stories are read. Despite the fact that the story is narrated by a suburbanite advertising man, the concerns of the narrator with the nature of reality and fiction align him more plausibly with the role of writer than with his assigned occupation. The narrator's name is Moses, he lives in Proxmire Manor, and his wife has a cousin Justina, all details which seem to make him Moses Wapshot, but there is nothing further in the story to identify him with the character of the Wapshot novels. As far as we know, Moses was not an advertising copywriter, he did not have the three brothers, all dead, who are referred to in this story, and, most important, he never was as perceptive and articulate in the novels as the narrator of this story is. Why Cheever does the little he does to remind us of Moses Wapshot is a mystery since he doesn't follow through by making any significant use of the character from an earlier work. The situation of the story involves cousin Justina's sudden death while visiting Moses's wife, only to have it develop that, thanks to overly rigid zoning laws, she cannot be buried from the house in which she had the bad taste to die. This grotesque situation provides, however, only a minimal narrative line for the story; actually the dilemma is solved quite simply when Moses threatens the mayor with the possibility that he will bury Justina in his garden and that proper official gives in and grants an exception. The main point of the story seems to be the narrator's extended reflection upon the world in which such absurdity happens. He begins the story with a passage that serves to introduce the events of this story and, in mood at least, of the entire collection:

So help me God it gets more and more preposterous, it corresponds less and less to what I remember and what I expect as if the force of life were centrifugal and threw one further and further away from one's purest memories and ambitions.... Fiction is art and art is the triumph over chaos (no less) and we can accomplish this only by the most vigilant exercise of choice, but in a world that changes more swiftly than we can perceive, there is always the danger that our powers of selection will be mistaken and that the vision we serve will come to nothing. We admire decency and we despise death but even the mountains seem to shift in the space of a night and perhaps the exhibitionist at the corner of Chestnut and Elm Streets is more significant than the lovely woman with a bar of sunlight in her hair, putting a fresh piece of cuttlebone in the nightingale's cage. (pp. 1–2)[6]

Anyone can be forgiven for feeling that we have here a writer of fiction rather than an advertising man addressing us. This passage is reminiscent of the statement of intent in the preface to this volume and certainly not a conventional beginning to a story. In addition to making this opening statement, the narrator reflects later on the situation of the world in which he lives in a way that again has nothing to do with the narrative itself:

I stand, figuratively, with one wet foot on Plymouth Rock, looking with some delicacy, not into a formidable and challenging wilderness but onto a half-finished civilization embracing glass towers, oil derricks, suburban continents and abandoned movie houses and wondering why, in this most prosperous, equitable, and accomplished world — where even the cleaning women practice the Chopin etudes in their spare time — everyone should seem to be so disappointed. (p. 8)

This passage looks forward to Melissa Wapshot's perception of universal boredom as it precipitates her fall from grace in Cheever's next book, *The Wapshot Scandal.* It is also reminiscent of Fitzgerald's awareness, as expressed in *The Great Gatsby,* that the frontier experience, however "formidable and challenging," offered a simpler arena for self-discovery and self-mastery than any available to his characters in the twentieth century. But Cheever, like Fitzgerald, warns against nostalgia as the solution to this disappointment in the present. Moses reflects at one point in this story, "I seemed to hear the jinglebells of the sleigh that would carry me to grandmother's house although in fact grandmother spent the last years of her life working as a hostess on an ocean liner and was lost in the tragic sinking of the *S.S. Lorelei* and I was responding to a memory that I had not experienced" (p. 9). Moses is here warning himself against the pervasiveness of a cultural mythology, which is harder and harder to square with the facts of either the past or the present. But the main observation of the story centers on the matter of the modern world's refusal to allow for essential facts like death — attempting to zone it out of Proxmire Manor altogether. As Moses thinks how Justina's funeral is conducted almost furtively, as if to die were a disgrace, he ponders: "How can a people who do not mean to understand death hope to understand love, and who will sound the alarm?" (p. 18). Cheever suggests no solutions to the dilemmas he delineates in this story — not even the meaningful connection to the past which was Coverly Wapshot's survival mechanism — only the sensibility of one observer and a clear sounding of the alarm.

The remaining stories — quite different from this one in tone and degree of social and philosophical commentary — can be divided into those set in America — "The Lowboy," "The Scarlet Moving Van," and "The Wrysons" — and those set in Italy, "The Duchess," "The Golden Age," and "Boy in Rome." The second story in the collection, "Brimmer," is neither or both; it involves an American traveling to Italy, and most of it takes place on board ship. The ordering of the stories — beginning with "Justina," with its general reflections on American culture in the twentieth century, followed by "Brimmer," which could be seen as a transition between America and the Old World, and then American stories alternating with Italian ones, ending with the essaylike "Miscellany of Characters That Will Not Appear" tempts one to try again to see some underlying novelistic structure to the whole. But it seems to me that the alternating pairs of American and Italian stories would need to have some relationship to each other to make for a satisfactory sense of unity, and they don't, really. It is difficult, in fact, to see any substantial unifying thread even among the three American stories or the three Italian stories themselves. I am inclined to let the search for some "novelistic" sense of unity drop and to consider that, at most, Cheever was exploring some situations and characters that he planned to "evict" from his future work, as he indicates in the little preface. Even here, it is hard to believe that he would want to evict sensibilities like those of Moses in "The Death of Justina" or the narrator of "Brimmer."

"Brimmer" resembles "The Death of Justina" in that the plot, such as it is, is outweighed by the narrator's observations and reactions. In this story, the narrator meets and is fascinated by Brimmer, a modern-day satyr, whom he meets on a ship to Italy. However indecent such character types are, the narrator points out that satyrs outnumber gods and heroes in Mediterranean statuary, a detail which seems to indicate that we should try to understand them. Bored on the ocean crossing, the narrator strikes up an acquaintance with the charming Brimmer, the pleasure of whose company he is to lose in turn to a charming Frenchwoman returning to her husband and children in Paris, a Roman businesswoman, and the daughter of an American family from the South. The narrator disapproves of this behavior, believing that such extreme promiscuity really reveals, in his words, "an especial degree of human failure. . . . I knew no one who had hit on such a way of life except as an expression of inadequacy — a shocking and repugnant unwillingness to cope with the generous forces of life" (p. 33). Yet, when they disembark, the narrator agrees to drive up to Rome with Brimmer and still another woman he has picked up. As they drive into Assisi, a sudden storm comes up. When they visit the duomo, a wind breaks the windows and extinguishes every candle. As they leave the town, the wind ceases and the sunlight returns. The narrator speculates that this is portentous, that nature or religion was making a moral judgment on Brimmer. Later, back in America, the narrator receives a forwarded letter from Brimmer's last companion, informing him that Brimmer is dying in Zurich and enclosing some papers that Brimmer had wanted him to have as "his best friend." The loneliness implicit in Brimmer's designating a shipboard acquaintaince as his best friend provokes the narrator's realization that he had suspected all along that Brimmer was dying, "that his promiscuity was a relationship not to life but to death" (p. 36). The papers turn out to include pornographic ramblings, a prayer for cleanliness of heart, a poem, the beginnings of a journal. The apparent death of Brimmer seems to lay to rest an uneasiness in the narrator's mind as he has wondered why Brimmer, with grace and intelligence, had failed: "Which of us is not suspended by a thread above carnal anarchy, and what is that thread but the light of day?" (p. 38). The narrator concludes that it has to do with self-control and a love of *all* life's pleasures, going on deck to see the landfall at Lisbon instead of staying in bed with a woman one has picked up. But a short time later his complacency is shattered. In Europe again, he sees a picture of Brimmer in a magazine, not dead but newly married to an Italian movie actress. His posture in the photograph is what the narrator remembers from shipboard, the classic pose of the satyr, right foot crossed in front of the left, glass full of the fruit of grape. The narrator's reaction is to feel oddly disoriented, "worlds away from home" (p. 39). Until the ending, the conflict between the narrator's moral code and Brimmer's promiscuity seems the point of the story. But why does the narrator need to think Brimmer dead in order to feel vindicated? Why is he so disturbed to find him alive? If there is a moral conflict within the narrator to which Brimmer's example speaks, that would explain his reaction, but if there is, it isn't made clear, and in fact it seems not to be the case. Apparently, the narrator is thrown by the discovery that someone without the values he believes to be life-enhancing can be charming, successful, a survivor in his own way. If the narrator's view is to provide the point of this story, it is unclear what we are left with at the end.

The three American stories are considerably better than the Italian ones, perhaps because they all deal with issues which have real resonance for Cheever. "The Lowboy" is another story about brothers, and also about one's relationship to the past, but Cheever takes a very different view of that connection from that in the Wapshot novels. This time the narrator's brother, Richard, is an unpleasant, spoiled, egocentric, possessive man. The story involves a fight over a piece of heirloom furniture from the brothers' family home; the narrator wants only one item, a lowboy. Richard wants it more — "so much more ... that there was no point in even discussing it" (p. 42). He claims to want it as the one thing that will remind him of his past; his brother suspects it's for cachet, for proof of his distinguished ancestry, as an artifact to appear in the background on Christmas card pictures. The narrator gives in, and Richard proceeds to restore the lowboy and then to place it on a rug exactly like the one it had stood on, to place on it a silver pitcher full of leaves exactly as in their childhood. The effect of this faithful restoration is to evoke the past in all its unhappiness. The narrator remarks that Richard "had been too late in realizing that the fascination of the lowboy was the fascination of pain, and he had committed himself to it" (p. 53). Driven back upon memories of his wretched childhood, Richard seems to revert in his behavior to that spoiled, unhappy child that he was. He quarrels with everyone at a Thanksgiving dinner in his home, just as in his childhood days, and the narrator goes home from this holiday fiasco and throws away the antiques and artifacts from the past which are in his own home. As he destroys this link to the past, he exclaims: "Dismiss whatever molests us and challenges our purpose, sleeping or walking. Cleanliness and valor will be our watchwords. Nothing less will get us past the armed sentry and over the mountainous border" (p. 56). This inflated language emphasizes the sense of the past as dangerous, a pitfall for the person who would live happily and purposefully in the present, a very different view of the past that we saw in the Wapshot novels. The difference would appear to be that Richard, in this story, reverts to the past itself, while Coverly Wapshot tries to retain only the meaningful, sustaining aspects of it which can be brought into the present. The point of "The Lowboy" seems to be that if one cannot build a usable bridge from the past to one's present, then one is better off totally free of the past, an interesting variation on a major Cheever theme.

"The Scarlet Moving Van" is set in an unnamed suburb, referred to only as "the unincorporated township of B—." The purpose of this deliberate vagueness of setting becomes clear when we realize that this is a story about human responsibility rather than an observation of the realistic manners of suburban life. The tone of the description of life in this suburb is the first clue to the fabulous nature of the story:

Life was unprecedentedly comfortable and tranquil. B— was exclusively for the felicitous... In nearly every house there were love, graciousness, and high hopes. The schools were excellent, the roads were smooth, the drains and other services were ideal, and one spring evening at dusk an immense scarlet moving van with gold lettering on its sides came up the street and stopped in front of the Marple house.... (p. 83)

The new neighbors of the protagonist, Charlie Folkestone, are Peaches and Gee-Gee, a couple whose external charm conceals a dire problem. After a few drinks, the handsome and personable Gee-Gee (for Greek God, his nickname in college) becomes critical and abusive and begins to remove his clothes and climb on the furniture. To his wife's entreaties of "not on our first night here," he replies "I have to teach them, honey.... They've got to learn." Peaches reveals that this is usual behavior, and that they have had to move eight times in the previous eight years. Their time in B— is limited to only a few months, and they move on. Charlie Folkestone puts up with them longest:

He felt he understood the drunken man's message; he had always sensed it. It was at the bottom of their friendship.... To the happy and the well-born and the rich he had this to say — that for all their affection, their comforts, and their privileges, they would not be spared the pangs of anger and lust and the agonies of death. . . . But was it not possible to accept this truth without having him dance a jig in your living room? He spoke from some vision of the suffering in life, but was it necessary to suffer oneself in order to accept his message? It seemed so. (p. 91)

Some months later, Charlie visits Gee-Gee in his new home; he has broken his leg and is trying to get around in a children's wagon, having sent his wife and family away for the holidays. Charlie leaves and drives home in a snowstorm, concerned that Gee-Gee might manage to burn the house down in his helpless state. Arrived home after a perilous drive and playing Vivaldi sonatas with his children as is their custom on Sunday, he is interrupted by a phone call from Gee-Gee, who has fallen out of his wagon and pleads that Charlie come and help him. Thinking of the storm and staring at his children's trusting faces, he hangs up the phone. That very night, tormented by guilt, he begins to drink. Soon he is drinking too much and quarreling with his wife, and "in the end, he lost his job, and they had to move, and began their wanderings, like Gee-Gee and Peaches, in the scarlet-and-gold van" (p. 102). That this mysterious role reversal is not necessary is made clear by the information we are given at the end of the story. It is not beside the point that after Charlie hung up, Gee-Gee called the local fire department who arrived in eight minutes flat, got him into bed and made him a fresh drink. The simplistic moral to which the story seems to be building — that one must not refuse to help others — is undercut by the revelation that the seemingly helpless Gee-Gee, who precipitates this fatal moral crisis for Charlie, is actually fairly self-sufficient and was, in this case, not in desperate need of help. Charlie's real failure is perhaps not so much the failure of humanity with which he charges himself but a failure of confident perception and discrimination as to where real need and real responsibility lie.

The last American story, "The Wrysons," is lighter in tone than the others. It involves a couple in Shady Hill whose obsession is zoning, whose mode is conformity, and who seem to live in fear that "there was a stranger at the gates . . . a man with a beard, a garlic breath, and a book" (p. 120). They seem particularly inflexible and not at all likable, but their concern about appearances masks private oddness. Irene Wryson has a recurrent dream that the hydrogen bomb has been dropped. The house is in a shambles, the sky is gray, and on the river people escaping in boats are ramming and shooting each other. At this point in her dream, she goes to the medicine cabinet, gets out a cyanide capsule for herself and her young daughter, only to drop them in the water and rubble in which she is standing. Then she wakes. She has never told her husband about her dream; nor has he told her *his* secret. He and his mother were abandoned by his father, and his most pleasant childhood memory has to do with her teaching him to bake — cookies, banana bread, even a Lady Baltimore cake. One day as a young man living alone in New York, he was overcome by depression; he relieved it by baking a Lady Baltimore cake:

> The next time he felt troubled, he resisted the temptation to bake a cake, but he was not always able to do this, and during the eight or nine years he had been married to Irene he must have baked eight or nine cakes. He took extraordinary precautions and she knew nothing of this. She believed him to be a complete stranger to the kitchen. And how could he at the breakfast table ... explain that he looked sleepy because he had been up until three baking a Lady Baltimore cake, which he had hidden in the garage? (p. 127)

One night Irene has her dream; she awakes to a sweet smell in the air and smoke in the hallway. Convinced that she is breathing atomic ash, she nevertheless goes downstairs, where she finds Donald asleep at the kitchen table and the room full of smoke. She wakes him.

> "I burned it," he said when he saw the smoke pouring from the oven. "I burned the damn thing."
> "I thought it was the hydrogen bomb," she said.
> "It's a cake," he said. "I burned it. What made you think it was the hydrogen bomb?"
> "If you wanted something to eat, you should have waked me," she said. (p. 129)

This moment, in which they are on the verge of learning something about each other, passes in this hilarious conversation of missed cues. "There were no further explanations. He threw the cake which was burned to a cinder, into the garbage, and they turned out the lights and climbed the stairs, more mystified by life than ever, and more interested than ever in a good appearance" (p. 130). Although it doesn't have the most serious subject or the most far-reaching theme of any story in this volume, "The Wrysons" is one of the best written. It builds cleverly to the crucial moment of missed communication in the kitchen and ends quickly and effectively with the couple exactly the same as they were at the beginning. It is more like the stories in *The Housebreaker of Shady Hill* wherein the crises are not, for the most part, tragic.

The Italian stories are considerably less successful; they all seem like sketches or vignettes, a form reminiscent of Cheever's earlier work. "The Duchess" involves the extraordinarily wealthy daughter of an Italian duke who is not impressed by her inheritance, nor by any of the impoverished nobles who would like to wed her and her money. Her father dies, her mother dies, and then she is free to do what she wishes — which is to marry Cecil Smith, the English clerk and bookkeeper who has worked for her family for years. Together they administer her fortune and live happily ever after. The ending can be seen coming a mile away, and the story is longer than the point requires. "The Golden Age" is even slighter. An American television writer has taken his family and himself to Italy because he is embarrassed to be a television writer and longs to do something more aesthetically noble: "He is in Italy only because he wants to lead a more illustrious life, to at least broaden his powers of reflection. He has even thought of writing a poem — something about good and evil" (p. 107). He has told the townspeople that he is a poet, believing that they will respect the role. Unfortunately, the situation comedy for which he wrote has made its way to Italian television; "The Best Family" is now to be seen as "La Famiglia Tosta." The night it begins, the writer's wife, children, and cook all go to the village to watch it; he stays behind apprehensively. Suddenly he sees his family returning, accompanied by the mayor, the doctor, a girl carrying flowers — a delegation. They congratulate him, and the major says: " 'Oh, we thought, *Signore,* that you were merely a poet' " (p. 118). This is like an O. Henry story whose only real point is to have a comic twist at the end.

"Boy in Rome" is the best of the Italian stories, probably because the main character is more fully developed than those of the other Italian stories, but it, too, is more a sketch than a well-developed narrative. It deals with an American boy who lives with his widowed mother in Rome; he used to spend summers in Nantucket but hasn't been back since his father died. The boy is experiencing adolescent *angst;* the line "I knew that I was never going to get all the loving I needed, no, never" echoes through the story. His situation is made worse by his mother's relative indifference to him, his father's death, and his foreign residence. He decides that what he really wants is to go back to Nantucket, and he gets a job to earn the money. One of his mother's friends involves him in a scheme to smuggle a valuable painting into the United States, which turns out to be a con game. The boy is not implicated, but he does miss his plane. The story ends with him still planning to get to America somehow or to some place where he will be understood. The story is really nothing more than a character sketch with a little attempt to make understandable nostalgia and the idealism that clings to the idea of America.

The last piece in the book is titled "A Miscellany of Characters that Will Not Appear" and consists of a list of characters or types that the author, speaking in his own voice here, vows not to use in his future work. William Peden notes that this section, really more essay than story, is "a moving manifesto and declaration of intent."[7] According to the "Miscellany," Cheever wants to eliminate from his fiction scenes of explicit sexual commerce, all parts for Marlon Brando, all lushes and homosexuals, and along with these:

All scornful descriptions of American landscapes with ruined tenements, automobile dumps, polluted rivers, jerry-built ranch houses, abandoned miniature golf links, cinder deserts, ugly hoardings, unsightly oil derricks, diseased elm trees, eroded farm lands, gaudy and fanciful gas stations, unclean motels, candle-lit tea-rooms, and streams paved with beer cans, for these are not, as they might seem to be, the ruins of our civilization, but are the temporary encampments and outposts of the civilization that we — you and I — shall build. (p. 165)

Yet, the jerry-built ranch houses and eroded farm lands will turn up in *The Wapshot Scandal;* the abandoned miniature golf links and diseased elm trees appear in *Bullet Park*. The operative word in the above eviction notice is "scornful"; when Cheever does use these things as part of the unavoidable landscape of his characters' real lives, it is without scorn and sometimes with a redeeming act of imaginative transformation. The other important thing in the above statement — as manifesto — is the last sentence; Cheever insists on the difference between declaring these things ruins of a deteriorating civilization and considering them temporary and improvable. And, at the same time that he rejects a scornful attitude toward the artifacts of modern life, Cheever also rejects the artistic escapes represented in the career of the fictional Royden

Blake, whom he discusses at the end of the "Miscellany." Blake's unexemplary career has included many dead-ends; he has tried simplistic moral anecdotes, snobbism, explicit sex, and at last a "romantic period." Cheever recounts the death-bed scene of this fictional author, in which he is still spinning one more trumped-up fantasy. Cheever asks how this sort of fiction can "hope to celebrate a world that lies spread out around us like a bewildering and stupendous dream?" (p. 175). Cheever is declaring his intent to avoid both scornful social commentary and escapist fantasy. He says that the world may be bewildering, the dream may verge on nightmare, but the writer must still approach the material of his times with the will to celebrate it.

This book is the darkest of Cheever's volumes thus far; in fact, one reviewer titled his review, "Cheever's Inferno." The view of the world in these stories is more ominous, less relieved by humor or celebration, than in Cheever's previous work. The suburbanites in this volume are not restored to a sense of joy and a firm possession of meaning in their lives as they were, for the most part, in the Shady Hill stories. The choice of the word "celebrate" in the author's last line in the "Miscellany" is more a statement of intent, for the future to be executed by an effort of the artist's will, than it is a description of what he has done in this volume. Perhaps we have to see the stories in this volume, most of them published first between 1955 and 1960, in relation to what Cheever has said about the decade of the Fifties itself:

The decade began for me with more promise than I can remember since my earliest youth. The war was over. Most of its reverberations were (for me) ended. . . . I could work in peace. However, halfway through the decade, something went terribly wrong. The most useful image I have today is of a man in a quagmire, looking into a tear in the sky. I am not speaking here of despair, but of confusion. I fully expected the trout streams of my youth to fill up with beer cans and the meadows to be covered with houses; I may even have expected to be separated from most of my moral and ethical heritage; but the forceful absurdities of life today find me unprepared. Something has gone very wrong, and I do not have the language, the imagery, or the concepts to describe my apprehensions. I come back again to the quagmire and the torn sky.[8]

It seems to me that the stories in this collection have been written out of a sense of the pervasive absurdity abounding in the world and a sense of confusion as to how to deal with it. What Cheever does seem to be able to do in these stories is to reject certain kinds of characters and *their* ways of coping with the confusion. He rejects Brimmer's lustfulness, the Wryson's blindness, Charlie Folkestone's unsubstantiated guilt. As one reviewer notes, in describing Cheever's announced intention to write people out of his system, "It is not so much their personalities Cheever rejects as their responses to life."[9] And in the "Miscellany" as well as the preface and the opening passage of "The Death of Justina," Cheever rejects certain artistic compromises and escapes as well.

CHAPTER 5

A Darker View: The Brigadier and the Golf Widow

THE collection *Some People, Places, and Things That Will Not Appear in My Next Novel* seems to represent, on Cheever's part, a break with certain subjects and techniques, that not only he had employed in his own work but that enjoyed a vogue in twentieth-century American literature generally. His next book, *The Wapshot Scandal,* seems to have completed a leave-taking from the author's own past, his family background and New England upbringing. Without exaggerating the degree of conscious departure from old themes, subjects, character types, and viewpoints marked by those two books, one can see a somewhat new direction in Cheever's next volume of short stories, *The Brigadier and the Golf Widow* (1964). There are, of course, obvious continuities with his previous work, and the vision of the world which will take vivid form in *Bullet Park* is slightly foreshadowed in a few stories. But this volume marks a real attempt on Cheever's part to deal directly and perhaps less gently than in the past with some of the dislocations he perceives in American society in the early 1960s, and a reader familiar with these stories, especially ones like "The Swimmer" and "The Music Teacher," will not be totally surprised by the quality of fable and the amount of violence that appears in *Bullet Park.*

William Peden feels that *The Brigadier and the Golf Widow* is probably Cheever's best volume of short stories.[1] I don't know that as a *volume* it is any better than *The Housebreaker of Shady Hill,* a collection of uniformly high quality. However, along with the Shady Hill anthology, this volume has provided the greatest number of frequently anthologized stories, including "The Swimmer," "The Angel of the Bridge," "Clementina," and "The Music Teacher." The stories in this volume are more varied than those in

91

the earlier ones, employing more different settings and more experiments in technique. For the first time in a collection of stories, a great number of them are primarily about women, a development which coincides with the featuring of Melissa in *The Wapshot Scandal*. Also, in this collection Cheever returns to the sketch as a form in several stories, including "Metamorphoses," "A Woman without a Country," "Reunion," and "A Vision of the World." These sketches, while lacking the impact of the stories with a strong narrative line, are considerably more dramatic and memorable than the sketches in earlier volumes. Stories set in American suburbs dominate the collection; there is also a group of stories about American expatriates — and in one case an Italian expatriate in America; and there is a small group of stories set in oceanside resorts. The last seem to combine elements of the first two types. The suburban stories are the most fully realized, but there is an unprecedented degree of variety among them, both in subject and in technique. If there is a unifying theme in this collection — and none ties all the stories together satisfactorily — it might be that of transformation or metamorphosis. Whereas in "The Enormous Radio" an object underwent a mysterious transformation in order to serve as an agent of initiation in the lives of the characters, in this volume a number of characters themselves undergo some sort of transformation, unsought, and often not for the better. The most obvious of such stories is the group of sketches titled "Metamorphoses" in which Cheever attempts an Ovidization of twentieth-century American lives, but stories like "The Swimmer" and "The Music Teacher" deal with this situation more convincingly.

The title story, "The Brigadier and the Golf Widow" is not a good example of the way in which Cheever will work the transformation idea in some of the stories; cataclysmic changes do occur in the lives of the characters, including financial reverses and divorce, but these changes proceed logically from the characters' own behavior. Nevertheless, the story sets the tone of the volume in its use of sudden, sweeping turnabouts in human lives. It is the most particularized in time of any Cheever story, taking its central situation from the bomb-shelter craze of the 1950s. Cheever is anxious, however, to integrate such data into his fiction without the fashionable distaste of tone that marked much socially critical literature of the early 1960s; his author/narrator speaks to his concern:

I would not want to be one of those writers who begin each morning by exclaiming, "O Gogol, O Chekhov, O Thackeray and Dickens, what would you have made of a bomb shelter ornamented with four plaster-of-Paris ducks, a birdbath, and three composition gnomes with long beards and red mob-caps? As I say, I wouldn't want to begin a day like this, but I often wonder what the dead would have done. But the shelter is as much a part of my landscape as the beech and horse-chestnut trees that grow on the ridge. (p. 1)[2]

Consequently, he tries to integrate this cultural detail into a story about human experience that transcends a particular moment in time. The danger, of course, is that a story with so recognizable a time-setting tends to be read narrowly as a piece of social satire; however, as in the Shady Hill stories, the events of the story and the human dynamics transcend the immediate moment. The story involves the marriage of the Pasterns. He is the brigadier of the country-club locker room, marching up and down yelling, "Bomb Cuba! Bomb Berlin! Let's throw a little nuclear hardware at them and show them who's boss" (p. 2). She is a typical suburban house-wife whose main mission is to collect money for fund-raising drives. Mr. Pastern has an affair with a neighborhood woman, who uses their relationship to blackmail him into giving her a key to their bomb-shelter. When Mrs. Pastern finds out about the affair, her response is warped by the nuclear paranoia of the time:

He had dragged her good name through a hundred escapades, debauched her excellence, and thrown away her love, but she had never imagined that he would betray her in their plans for the end of the world.... What could she do? She couldn't go back to Mother. Mother didn't have a shelter.... And then she remembered the night — the night of judgment — when they had agreed to let Aunt Ida and Uncle Ralph burn, when she had sacrificed her three-year-old niece and he his five-year-old nephew; when they had conspired like murderers and had decided to deny mercy even to his old mother. (p. 17)

This story captures the state of mind fostered by the threat of the hydrogen bomb and the workings of Dulles brinksmanship as well as any written in this period. But the story is most concerned with the inner dislocations of lives, whatever external rumblings may cause them. At the end we learn that Mr. Pastern is in jail for larceny, committed to pay the $38,000 bill for the bomb shelter, his wife and family are on home relief, and the neighbors are divorced.

The story is finally about human folly; the instances of it in this story are precipitated by preoccupation with the end of the world, but the victims are brought down mostly by their own inadequate responses to that threat of annihilation. The story sets the mood of the rest of the volume in that many others will deal with the clash between outer events and the individual's inner response to them.

The most famous story in the volume and the best example of Cheever's use of mysterious transformations is "The Swimmer." The only Cheever story ever made into a movie, it seems an odd choice because of its surrealistic quality. In the story Neddy Merrill, a resident of Bullet Park, sitting by a swimming pool on a Sunday afternoon listening to people talk about their hangovers, decides to invest the day with a heroic quality by swimming home, using the pools of his Westchester County neighbors. It should be noted that Sunday is the most dangerous day in Cheever's stories, probably because of its indeterminate nature. It is no longer part of the week-end with its social rituals, nor is it yet part of the week with its routines. It is the day on which people fall through their cracks in their lives. It is the day Cash Bentley dies in "O Youth and Beauty!," and it is the inevitable time setting for this story. In order that we not write off Neddy's plan as a prank or juvenile showing off, the narrator tells us: "He was not a practical joker nor was he a fool but he was determinedly original and had a vague and modest idea of himself as a legendary figure" (p. 62). We are to see Neddy's swim as an attempt to imaginatively transform the circumstances of his life — Sunday hangovers and lawn-to-lawn swimming pools — into something heroic. However, the story turns around, and a different sort of transformation occurs. At first the trip goes well; Neddy swims pool after pool, portaging through hedges and over manicured lawns. But a rainstorm stops him, and afterwards everything seems darker and different. There is suddenly an autumnal chill in the air. The Lindleys' riding ring is overgrown with weeds, although Neddy doesn't remember their selling the horses. The Welchers' pool is dry, odd for the summer. Trying to cross the freeway, he is laughed at and jeered; a beer can is thrown at him. At the Hallorans' he is consoled for his misfortunes, none of which he remembers. Leaves are now falling, and he smells woodsmoke; he is confused by these unseasonable phenomena. At the Sachses', there is a mention of an operation he cannot remember. The Biswangers, far beneath him in social status, are openly rude to him. His former mistress is hostile and says that she will lend him no more money. Smelling fall flowers and noticing autumn constellations in the sky, Neddy is disoriented and begins to cry, for the first time in his adult life, bewildered by the dislocations of seasons and the rudeness of his hosts. Dragging himself through the last two pools on his route and up the driveway of his home, he finds the house dark. No one has lived there for some time. This story is reminiscent of some of Hawthorne's in the reader's difficulty in ascertaining exactly what has happened. Did Neddy really make the swim? Why were his hosts early in the journey cordial and those later rude? The story cannot record the events of a single afternoon. Then is it pure fantasy? If so, it is set in a disconcertingly mimetic world. The real point of the story is the juxtaposition of the celebratory motive of Neddy's act with the social realities that emerge as the story progresses, realities that have to do with the role wealth and social status play in this world which Neddy wishes to invest with legendary beauty and meaning. The abruptness of the ending leaves us haunted by this story. Whatever "happened," we have seen a brightly lit, intelligible, comfortable world suddenly become dark and cold. The story, like a nightmare, leaves the reader with a residual uneasiness.

"The Angel of the Bridge" is a story that makes clearest Cheever's method in this volume because it proceeds from a familiar theme in the author's work, brotherly rivalry, but adds a supernatural element as it goes along. The story opens with the narrator telling about his seventy-eight-year-old mother, who, to his embarrassment, skates at Rockefeller Center, behavior which he does, however, understand as symptomatic of her nostalgia for the simple world of St. Botolphs where she grew up. The degree to which she is disconcerted by the modern world is revealed in her fear of airplanes. The narrator is less sympathetic to his brother's phobia about heights. The competitiveness of their relationship and the narrator's own proud freedom from neuroses prevents him from really empathizing, that is, until he himself develops a phobia about bridges. From that point on, he is beset by the dual need to avoid bridges and to conceal his malady from his family. His doctor is no help, and his own willpower is insufficient to get him across the massive bridges around New York City. Finally he recognizes his own phobia as the symptom of his dismay about the contemporary world, just as in the case with his mother. He had thought he could accommodate to the excesses of his own time, but now he realizes:

The truth is, I hate freeways and Buffalo Burgers. Expatriated palm trees and monotonous housing developments depress me.... I detest the destruction of familiar landmarks. I am deeply troubled by the misery and drunkenness I find among my friends, I abhor the dishonest practices I see. And it was at the highest point in the arc of a bridge that I became aware suddenly of the depth and bitterness of my feelings about modern life, and of the profoundness of my yearning for a more vivid, simple, and peaceable world. (p. 32)

This insight doesn't resolve his fear, but it does increase his sympathy for his mother and brother. One day he gets to the middle of a bridge and can go no farther. At this moment, the door opens and a girl with a harp enters his car and thanks him for picking her up. She tells him she's a folksinger, and she sings and plays the harp for him, soothing him and allowing him to complete the crossing without fear. He drives home in a world that has been restored to him and contemplates calling his brother on the chance that there is also an angel of elevators, but he fears that the detail of the harp will make him seem ridiculous or mad. Eschewing simple social satire in this story, Cheever instead deals with the idea that the transformations of the modern world make life an arena of psychic pitfalls. Mysterious and supernatural interventions may come to our aid, but the salvation is not extended to all sufferers and may be of only limited efficacy.

A similar pattern operates in "The Music Teacher." A traumatic transformation in the outward circumstance of the narrator is resolved by an almost supernatural intervention. The initial problem in Seton's life is that his wife has, through some inarticulated discontent, transformed herself into a hag. She deliberately burns the dinner, allows the children to ruin the furniture, and generally punishes him for their marriage. The motive for this transformation is not clear; her life is not filled with drudgery and her husband loves her: "It was like some subterranean sea change, some sexual campaign or revolution stirring — unknown perhaps to her — beneath the shining and common appearance of things" (p. 187). The story looks forward interestingly to issues in the women's movement, and the wife's destructive way of expressing her discontent is balanced by the prideful and unimaginative handling of the situation by her husband. Finally, one of his friends, noticing the disarray of their marriage, suggests that he needs a hobby — specifically piano lessons from a Miss Deming. Seton discovers when he goes to her house that her other pupils are also middle-aged men, all of whom take pains to conceal their identities. Miss Deming gives him an exercise to practice, and she continues to assign the same melody to him week after week. Finally his wife asks if he could convince his teacher to give him a new piece, and he asks her. Miss Deming responds that the wives *always* ask that and says:

> None of the gentlemen who come here have ever complained about my methods. . . . Of course, Mr. Purvis went too far. Mrs. Purvis is still in the sanitarium, but I don't think the fault is mine. You want to bring her to her knees, don't you? (p. 196)

Seton suddenly realizes that he is involved with some sort of witchcraft. As he walks home, he hears the mysterious melody coming from several homes in the neighborhood. Despite his doubts, the witchcraft obviously works; his wife pleads with him not to practice and reverts back to the loving woman she once was. Restored to a world of edible dinners and domestic happiness, Seton now feels disgust at the thought of Miss Deming, who turns up dead one night in a lonely place in the country. The mystery of her death underlines the supernatural power of the melody which — despite Seton's ambivalence — has healed his marriage. The story is effective except for the final scene of the piano teacher's death, which really doesn't add to our sense of her mysteriousness. The story is memorable for its perceptive treatment of a sexual struggle for supremacy within a marriage and the oddly convincing intervention of witchcraft, which is no more mysterious finally than the initial crisis which sent Seton off to take piano lessons.

"The Music Teacher," as we saw, tied together two motifs in this volume, the role of women in middle-class American society and the presence of almost supernatural powers in the world. "An Educated American Woman" focuses more directly on the issue of women — and more negatively. Jill Chidchester Madison, a precocious girl with a fancy education, is married to "an unintellectual 190-pound halfback," as she writes to her alumnae magazine, and is the mother of a young son, Bibber. She has filled her life with the presidencies in turn of all the civic organizations in town and has also managed a travel agency for nine months while its owner was ill. People admiring the Madison home do not know that the furniture and silverware have been polished by Georgie, her husband,

not because he enjoys housework but because he loves his wife and
sees that her self-concept doesn't really allow for household chores.
He also takes on most of the child-care responsibilities out of a profound love for his son. One summer Jill organizes a tour to Venice;
Georgie is to join her there at the end, which necessitates sending
Bibber to summer camp. The boy is miserable; and when Georgie
gets to Venice, Jill takes him on a frenetic tour of cathedrals and
palaces, as though she has forgotten the tour is finished. The juxtaposition of Bibber's unhappiness and Jill's inappropriate behavior
sets up the climax of the story. While Jill is out on one occasion,
Bibber becomes ill and the babysitter leaves him alone. The boy
dies. To this point, the behavior of Jill has seemed clearly intoler-
able; she is likely to recite in French paragraphs of a book she is
writing on Flaubert during a moment of lovemaking with her husband. But a narrator takes over at this point and seems to be more
critical of Georgie than of Jill. Georgie gets a divorce and the
narrator says: "Georgie was crushed by the death of his son. He
blamed Jill, which was cruel and unreasonable and it seemed, in the
end, that he could be both" (p. 59). We learn that Jill has a job
with a publishing firm in Cleveland and that Georgie ends up bitter
toward women and with a tendency to drink too much. The narrator, after taking down his phone number, throws it away at the end
of the story. This negative attitude toward Georgie — who has
seemed to be through the story very long-suffering in the face of
Jill's behavior — is hard to understand, and the ending of the story
is disconcerting. Reexamining the story, there still seems very little
reason to sympathize with Jill, except that she has an unmaternal
mother who gives her little encouragement in the development of
her emotional nature and who emphasizes a separation between
matters intellectual and domestic. Consequently, the story's ending
— with its apparent criticism of the husband — seems at variance
with the feelings most readers would have about the characters'
behavior in the story. Until the ending, we have one of Cheever's
most unflattering portraits of the modern American woman.

   The other stories that use the suburban milieu as setting and
thematic focus — "Metamorphoses," "Marito in Citta," and
"The Ocean" — are less significant. The first is a series of sketches
based on Ovidian antecedents and utilizing surprise endings. A
character named Harry Actaeon is, like his classical parallel, torn
apart by his own dogs; an Orpheus figure, who sings commercials,
loses his Eurydice. The stories are a bit heavy-handed in their classi-

cism and sketchy in their development. They provide the most obvious use of the device of mysterious transformations in this volume. "Marito in Città" is a predictable story of a man who has a summer fling while his wife is away; he becomes involved with a woman who offers to cook for him because he is starving due to his own lack of culinary skill. "The Ocean," like "The Music Teacher," involves a battle between the sexes; a man believes his wife is trying to poison him since she several times seems to be sprinkling insecticide on his dinner. The story ends with an unconvincingly affirmative dream from which the man awakens filled with an oceanic love for everyone, wanting to write "luve" with a laundry marker on the walls and appliances. This is an unsatisfactory ending; for all we know, his wife *is* trying to kill him, and his moments of mystical transport may indeed be numbered. None of these stories, though set in familiar territory, are in the same class with the other suburban stories.

The Brigadier and the Golf Widow also contains three stories that deal with expatriation: "Clementina," "The Bella Lingua," and "A Woman without a Country." The last two are nothing more than sketches, both involving American women living abroad. In "The Bella Lingua" Kate Dresser lives in Rome with her teenaged son who wants nothing more than to go back to live in Iowa with relatives. She lives in an apartment in a palace which she can afford only because she allows the Duke of Rome and his friends to traipse through her quarters once or twice a week on their way to visit his sister. Her uncle comes, her son returns to America, but Kate remains in Italy, giving Italian lessons to other expatriates and preferring the limited glamour of life in Italy to none at all in Iowa. "A Woman without a Country" is more fantastic. Anne Tonkin was once a happily married suburbanite, but through a series of accidents involving driving her husband to the train while she was wearing a transparent negligee, running out of gas, being rescued by a neighbor who then took advantage of her, only to be discovered by her husband, who came back for his briefcase, she has lost both husband and child. During the custody battle she blamed her indiscretion on being drowsy due to the humidity, and this testimony turned up in newspaper headlines and even inspired a popular song, "Humid Isabella." She flees this derision and goes to Europe where she becomes one of those wandering American expatriates "who go to bed night after night to dream of bacon-lettuce-and-tomato sandwiches" (p. 157). She is homesick and

finally decides to go back, even planning where she will eat her first
BLT. However, the first thing she hears when disembarking is a
mechanic singing "Humid Isabella," and she catches the next plane
back to Europe and resumes her wanderings. Neither of these
stories throws much light on the real reasons that people become
expatriates, but both capture a little of the way of life involved.

"Clementina," a much-anthologized story, deals more inten-
sively with this subject. A double expatriation is involved; first we
see Americans in Europe who hire Clementina to do chores and
then help her with the heaviest work and in other ways upset her
sense of the propriety of their arrangements. Then, Clementina
becomes an expatriate when she returns with the family to
America. The point of the story seems to be the conflict between
Clementina's two worlds, the one in which she has grown up where
mystery and miracles are everyday matters and one of her cousins is
respected for having seen the devil and the American society where
machines do everything for her. In America an older Italian man
proposes to her, but she doesn't consider his proposal seriously
until her visa expires. Faced with a return to Italy, for which she is
intermittently homesick, she realizes the dimensions of her plight.
She visualizes her return to her village, the townspeople gathered
around, drinking wine and listening to her tales of frying pans with
brains and sweet-smelling cleaning powder:

> ...but then she saw gathering in the imagined faces of her townsmen a
> look of disbelief. Who would believe her tales? Who would listen? They
> would have admired her if she had seen the Devil, like Cousin Maria, but
> she had seen a sort of paradise and no one cared. In leaving one world and
> coming to another she had lost both. (p. 146)

Now, rereading letters from home, details of the hardships of life in
her village jump out at her. She decides to marry Joe, which causes
a breach between her and the man for whom she works since he
feels she should marry for love. She is mystified at this notion,
coming from a part of the world where the only really acceptable
motive for marriage is that the families of the couple own adjoining
land. She makes a satisfactory, if not ecstatic, marriage and is
vindicated later when she learns that her employer is divorced. So
much for love, she thinks, but the news reminds her again of the
world she has left behind, and "she wondered why the good God
had opened up so many choices and made life so strange and

diverse'' (p. 155). The story, told through Clementina's viewpoint, becomes both a comic commentary on American manners and a sympathetic rendering of the pull of two worlds on her.

The seaside stories — ''The Chaste Clarissa,'' ''A Vision of the World,'' and ''The Seaside Houses'' — are also, except for the last, less memorable than the suburban stories. ''The Chaste Clarissa'' is essentially a comic story about summer dalliance. A predatory summer boarder fails in his attempt to seduce a beautiful woman until he realizes that everyone has always admired her beauty — which is extraordinary — but disparaged her mind — which is less than ordinary. He flatters her about her intelligence and begs to hear some of her opinions; she begins to express one inane opinion after the other, and ''it was as simple as that'' (p. 184). The story is light entertainment, very well executed. ''A Vision of the World'' involves a man's sense that the world is changing in incoherent ways, a similar perception to that of the narrator in ''The Angel of the Bridge.'' He feels that compared to events around him, his dreams are orderly and conservative. He begins to have a dream about some foreign phrase that has an incantational power over him but whose meaning he doesn't know. Finally, one night he wakes, sits up, and exclaims, ''Valor! Love! Virtue! Compassion! Splendor! Kindness! Wisdom! Beauty!'' He suddenly feels hopeful, contented, and at peace with the world which has been troubling him. The story is almost completely unrealized and hence it is hard to be uplifted by the narrator's newfound tranquillity.

''The Seaside Houses,'' on the other hand, is an excellent story, on a par with most of the best suburban stories in the volume. It deals with an idea that has appeared before in Cheever's fiction, namely, that people leave their presences in rooms and houses. This story also makes clear the way in which seaside cottages provide a sort of combination of the suburban and expatriate motifs found in other stories in this volume: mostly suburbanites rent them, but in doing so, the narrator of this story says: ''There is the sense that we are, as in our dreams we have always known ourselves to be, migrants and wanderers — travelers, at least, with a traveler's acuteness of feeling'' (p. 200). The narrator is sensitive to the presence of previous occupants, aware that sometimes people have been happy in a cottage and that then ''we rent their happiness as we rent their beach and their catboat'' (p. 201). And sometimes in the middle of the night, a door blows open suddenly, and his wife, half-asleep, says, ''Oh, why have they come back? . . . What have they lost?'' (p. 202). In this story, however, such acuteness of feeling leads to disaster. The narrator is attuned to the presence of Mr. Greenwood, the owner of the cottage he is renting. He discovers the man's secrets from clues like hidden whiskey bottles and a poignant note scrawled on the baseboard of the children's room: "My father is a rat. I repeat. My father is a rat" (p. 204). The narrator also learns from a neighbor of violent marital quarrels and other family disappointments. The sensitive narrator, a favorite Cheever type, feels a growing empathy and almost anxiety about Mr. Greenwood. One night he dreams about searching for liquor and wakes up feeling that he has dreamed one of Greenwood's dreams. In town on business, he sees Greenwood in a bar, recognizing him from photographs in the house. Sure enough, Greenwood turns out to be a drunk who becomes more abusive as the evening wears on. The narrator returns from this trip upset and immediately gets into a quarrel with his wife, one which ends abruptly:

> "Oh, God, you bore me this morning," my wife said.
> "I've been bored for the last six years," I said.
> I took a cab to the airport, and an afternoon plane to the city. We had been married twelve years and had been lovers for two years before our marriage . . . and I never saw her again. (p. 212)

This story not only uses the theme of transformation that appears in many of the stories in this volume, but is also reminiscent of "The Scarlet Moving Van": in both stories observant, increasingly involved bystanders end up becoming like the person they were observing. In this story, the narrator is transformed by an imaginative understanding of Greenwood, which leads him mysteriously to assume some of Greenwood's qualities. This development is a little frightening; it seems that the narrator's best quality, his empathetic response to human suffering, results in his own negative metamorphosis.

This volume contains some memorable stories. The experiments with fable as a form which commence in the *People, Places, and Things* volume come to fruition here, with particular success in "The Swimmer" and "The Music Teacher" and "The Seaside Houses." Cheever's starting point is still a mimetic representation of the world as in the Shady Hill collection, but as one reviewer said, "In John Cheever's world, the matter-of-fact reality of contemporary life trips abruptly over its own ordinariness. Conventions and normality suddenly tumble, word by word, into a fantastical surreal setting. . . . No moment, no person, no one of a thousand details of modern life is too innocent and ordinary to escape his power to charge it sinisterly."³ The best stories of this volume do exactly that, and they prepare us somewhat for the fantastic events and sinister forces that appear in *Bullet Park*.

CHAPTER 6

Bullet Park: *Shady Hill with Sniper*

IN his introduction to the anthology *Fiction of the Fifties,* Herbert Gold describes life in the contemporary world in these words:

We are in the shoes of the man poised on the edge of the cliff, deciding about life and mortality, who finally sighs and turns away, resolute against suicide. He will live! There is only one chance for a man, and it is here on earth! ... At that moment he is shot in the chest by a mad sniper.[1]

Gold goes on to delineate the role of the writer in such a world: "He must celebrate and value experience. He must see clearly. He must relish what he sees. He must make sense. *And he must not forget the snipers.*"[2] This passage provides a helpful access route to an understanding of the place of *Bullet Park* (1969), Cheever's third novel, in his career. Cheever's work has always been marked by celebration, clear vision, and good sense. But Cheever's description of his sense of the world of the late 1950s as a place of quagmires and a torn sky — images, he said, of confusion — is no longer adequate to his vision; the world of the late 1960s, if one is to judge from this novel, is downright dangerous. Some of the stories in *The Brigadier and the Golf Widow,* which appeared between the second Wapshot novel and this one, prepare for this sense of dislocation and danger, but it is in *Bullet Park* that Cheever's world becomes ominous. We have traveled from the relative calm and restorable tranquillity of Shady Hill, through the absurd and puzzling Proxmire Manor, where zoning laws make it illegal to die, to Bullet Park, where madness and death are more prominent than ever before in Cheever's fiction. He has not relinquished the sense of the promise of life which certain sensitive characters apprehend in the ordered suburban world of his other works, but the elements which legislate against happiness, and even survival, are more present and more terrible. Some characters in this novel try to sustain a belief in life in *Bullet Park* as paradisiacal, but the world of this suburb is, as Samuel Coale says, a "Lethal Eden."[3]

No work of Cheever's has been received with less critical consensus than *Bullet Park*. By the time it appeared, Cheever's prestige was sufficient to warrant the lead review in the *New York Times,* but in that review Benjamin DeMott generally discounted the achievement of this novel. He was unmoved by Cheever's handling of subject and characterization in the work and very troubled by the structural problem he perceived, calling the book "broken-backed" and "tacked together."[4] Mary Ellmann charged Cheever with writing about "fashionable pain" and the "moral insufficiency of power mowers and martinis."[5] Samuel Coale, while acknowledging that this is Cheever's most experimental and carefully created novel, also feels that the book is too episodic and suggests that the style of the novel is too light for the darkness of the vision it communicates.[6] The most favorable and, I think, perceptive review that appeared at the time of the novel's publication was in *Time* magazine. The reviewer immediately saw that the novelist was much less interested in the manners and morals of suburbia than in ancient religious and philosophical concerns with good and evil, chance and accident, will and fate.[7] It remained for John Gardner, in a retrospective essay published in 1971, to give the book its rightful place in Cheever's *oeuvre* and in twentieth-century fiction. Announcing that the critics who had dismissed the novel when it was published were "dead wrong," he asserts: "The Wapshot books, though well-made, were minor. 'Bullet Park,' illusive, mysteriously built, was major — in fact, a magnificent work of fiction." He feels that the novel was misunderstood for several reasons, including the fact that it refuses to articulate a simple message and also, he says, because "Cheever is right about evil; it comes quietly, unannounced by thunder or screeching bats." He apparently expects that readers will not easily take seriously the handling of evil in the novel because of the way that Cheever depicts it. Gardner also understands that *Bullet Park* is a philosophical novel about chance rather than a novel of manners about American suburban life. He suggests, furthermore, that it is Cheever's handling of *voice* which makes that novel as effective as he believes it is. His final guess as to why reviewers were annoyed by the novel sums up his sense of its value:

> The novel is bleak, full of danger and offense, like a poisoned apple in the playpen. Good and evil are real, but are effects of mindless chance — or heartless grace.... A religious book, affirmation out of ashes.... The image repetitions, the stark and subtle correspondences that create the book's ambiguous meaning, its uneasy courage and compassion, sink in and in, like a curative spell.[8]

I agree with Gardner's assessment — his experience of *Bullet Park* seems to have been much like mine — and I disagree particularly with the bases of the negative response that greeted the book's publication. *Bullet Park* is not marred by serious structural problems; far from taking a chic critical view of the suburbs, it is not even *about* life in suburbia; and the style seems well suited to the content, especially if one thinks in terms of Gardner's observations about Cheever's use of voice. It is as well constructed, thematically provocative, and fictionally successful a novel as Cheever has written.

Some initial difficulties confront, however, any reader who innocently picks up *Bullet Park,* and perhaps bother most those familiar with Cheever's earlier work. The story involves two characters named Hammer and Nailles, and understandably these names initially struck many readers and reviewers as gimmicky and certainly worked against the seriousness with which such readers were willing to take the novel. The plot involves the mysterious illness of Nailles's son Tony, who refuses to get out of bed one morning, and its equally mysterious cure by a swami; the plan of Hammer to crucify Nailles on the altar of Christ Church, a plan later revised to make Tony the victim; and the sudden phobia about riding commuter trains that turns Nailles, the best-adjusted character in the novel, into a drug addict. Such a plot obviously doesn't make it easy for the reader to feel on firm, serious ground. Is it an allegory? Is it a joke? Fate has intervened before in Cheever's suburban world; certain accidents, some happy, some unfortunate, have befallen his characters; but the circumstances have not usually been so bizarre nor the consequences so dire. However, even the extreme degree to which chance is the dominant force in this novel is made to work effectively, and for two identifiable reasons. First, Cheever sets these coincidences, mad plots, and potential tragedies within a world which is presented to us with enough verisimilitude to make us reasonably comfortable. Second, although he retains the high degree of omniscience that has come to mark his storytelling mode, except for Part Two of the novel — which is turned over entirely to Hammer's journal — he allows us more insight than usual in his fiction into the characters' minds, backgrounds, dreams, and motives. The effect of this knowledge of the interior nature of the characters — at least of Hammer and Nailles — is to make much of what occurs in the novel seem humanly possible if not always logically plausible.

The attempt to provide the reader with the security of a verisimilar world begins on the opening pages of the novel:

Paint me a small railroad station then, ten minutes before dark. Beyond the platform are the waters of the Wekonsett River, reflecting a somber after glow. The architecture of the station is oddly informal, gloomy but unserious, and mostly resembles a pergola, cottage or summer house although this is a climate of harsh winters. The lamps along the platform burn with a nearly palpable plaintiveness. The setting seems in some way to be at the heart of the matter. (p. 3)[9]

The rest of the first chapter involves the arrival by train of a man, who turns out later to be Hammer, to be met by a real-estate agent and shown around Bullet Park and finally taken to see a house. This device allows the reader to tour Bullet Park and get a sense of its physical being as well as its social dimensions. To provide the latter, Cheever then gives us a seriocomic picture of the Wickwires, people whose engagement calendar is booked solid from Labor Day to the Fourth of July: "They were quite literally social workers — celebrants — using their charm and their brilliance to make things go at a social level" (p. 6). In the effort they exhaust and sometimes even injure themselves physically; it is as though they have turned their social mission into almost a religious sacrificial rite. Throughout the novel Cheever continues to cite the routines of suburban life — parties, commuter trains, volunteer fire companies, chain saws, Sunday mornings at church — to allow the reader some sense of a credible world in which the events of the novel *could* occur.

Furthermore, the view of suburban life in the novel is complex. In the first chapter, we are given the critical view of an angry unnamed adolescent:

Damn the bright lights by which no one reads, damn the continuous music which no one hears, damn the grand pianos that no one can play, damn the white houses mortgaged up to their rain gutters, damn them for plundering the ocean for fish to feed the mink whose skins they wear and damn their shelves on which there rests a single book — a copy of the telephone book bound in pink brocade. (p. 5)

The excessiveness of this passage undermines it, and the narrator rejects his view, saying that "the adolescent, as adolescents always are, would be mistaken" (p. 6). Right here the novel is saved from Ellmann's charge that it involves a cheap, fashionable criticism of suburban life. However, Cheever does also provide some comic exaggerations which touch on the real excesses of suburban life. For instance, there are the Ridleys —

a couple who brought to the hallowed institution of holy matrimony a definitely commercial quality.... They were not George and Helen Ridley. They were "the Ridleys." One felt that they might have incorporated and sold shares in their destiny over the counter. "The Ridleys" was painted on the door of their station wagon. There was a sign saying "The Ridleys" at the foot of their driveway. In their house, matchbooks, coasters and napkins were all marked with their name. They presented their handsome children to their guests with the air of salesmen pointing out the merits of a new car in a showroom. The lusts, griefs, exaltations and shabby worries of a marriage never seemed to have marred the efficiency of their organization. One felt that they probably had branch offices and a staff of salesmen on the road. (pp. 100–101)

Or there is Tommy Lewellen, invitations to whose parties read: "The Amalgamated Development Corporation and Mr. and Mrs. Thomas Lewellen cordially request the pleasure..." so that he can deduct the cost of the party on his income tax. Nailles, who generally loves his suburban life, does have moments of restiveness, one when he is dressing for a party: "He did not cherish his nakedness but he detested his suit. Spread out on the bed it seemed to claim a rectitude and a uniformity that was repulsively unlike his nature" (p. 240). But for the most part, the novel's attitude toward the suburbs is not negative; its gist is expressed in this statement Nailles makes to his son:

When you go to the theater they're always chopping at the suburbs but I can't see that playing golf and raising flowers is depraved. The living is cheaper out here and I'd be lost if I couldn't get some exercise. People seem to make some connection between respectability and moral purity that I don't get. For instance, the fact that I wear a vest doesn't necessarily mean that I claim to be pure in heart. . . . All kinds of scandalous things happen everywhere but just because they happen to people who have flower gardens doesn't mean that flower gardens are wicked. (p. 66)

Nailles is not Cheever's spokesman in the novel, and, in fact, his loves and enthusiasms are almost simplistic; but the sanity of his view that suburbs are simply places to live which offer certain options for the use of one's time rather than symbols of moral probity is hard to argue. Despite the fact that the novel's focus is not on the manners of suburban life, Cheever does give us a clearly delineated arena — which happens to be suburban — in which his characters live and the events occur. And perhaps *because* he is anxious that the reader get past the issue of suburbia, its merits and defects, to the novel's underlying concern with good and evil, accident and will, he has taken pains to complicate his portrait of suburbia so that the reader has to see it as the same mixture of positive and negative possibilities that marks any terrain where people live their lives.

Along with placing the admittedly fabulous events of the novel in a believable setting, Cheever gives credibility to the novel by revealing the interior of his major characters to a degree unusual for him, seemingly to make the reader conclude that even if the characters' behavior appears incredible in the normal course of events, it does proceed somewhat plausibly from their inner workings. The main developments in the lives of the two main characters are that Nailles becomes a drug addict while Hammer plans and tries to execute a sacrificial murder. Oddly enough, the latter is almost easier to believe than the former, because it turns out that Hammer is insane, and there is a certain mad logic in some of his behavior that does not cover the behavior of Nailles.

Hammer arrives at his mental instability by an understandable route. He is the illegitimate son of a wealthy socialist, who never acknowledges him, and Gretchen Schurz, a midwestern girl who had become the father's secretary. He is raised by his paternal grandmother, who only agrees to take him because of his blond hair (which turns brown when he is seven). While trying to decide on a legal name, the grandmother looks out the window as the gardener walks by carrying a hammer; she settles on Paul Hammer. He never sees his father; and his visits to his mother are unsatisfactory as she becomes crazier and crazier, convinced that she hears Brahms concertos in the noise of airplane engines and that she can ascertain the nature of the people who occupied hotel rooms before she did. In one of her rambling monologues, she suggests to Paul that he crucify a comfortable suburbanite in order to wake up a drugged world. Hammer struggles on alone through adolescence and early manhood, one day waking up in the grip of a cafard — a palpable melancholy or despair — for which he concludes the only remedy will be to live in a room with yellow walls. He travels from city to city, country to country, finally spotting his salvation in a house in Blenville, Pennsylvania. The divorcee who owns the house doesn't want to sell it, but she is killed in an accident which is ambiguously Hammer's fault, and he buys the house and moves in. He falls in love with a woman in the neighborhood because she has a white thread on her collar; their marriage isn't happy because she will only sleep with him during thunderstorms or other convulsions of nature or history. He and Marietta move to Bullet Park, where she, like Gee-Gee in "The Scarlet Moving Van," denounces the hypocrisy of suburban life to Hammer's murmured "Not tonight, dear. Not so soon." One day, remembering his mother's suggestion, he begins to plot the crucifixion of Eliot Nailles. He learns about him in a dental magazine (Nailles manufactures mouthwash), and he is affected by the coincidence of their names; there is no better reason than this for his choice. Later, he decides to kill Tony instead, for no clearer reason. Hammer is somewhat aware of his plight. Once on a beach he was propositioned by a homosexual and avoided the encounter by helping a family launch a kite. He realizes later that he has married a piece of thread on a collar and been saved by a kite string, and he longs for a world with more substantial meaning and order. There is an internal logic to much of what Hammer does as well as moments at which his life could have gone differently had chance led in another direction. The degree of chance in the events which lead to his final act — from his birth to his marriage to his moving to Bullet Park and meeting a man named Nailles — is very strong. Furthermore, the way in which we receive the details of Hammer's life strengthens our sense of his madness; this data is conveyed through Hammer's journal, the tone of which is cold and matter-of-fact when we would expect anger, pain, and perhaps some guilt. As Gardner says, "The rendered proof of his demonic nature is his voice, a quiet stovelid on terror and rage."[10] Part Two of *Bullet Park,* entirely given over to Hammer's journal, is effective because it builds some motivation for an almost inexplicable act and also because the manner of the telling increases both the credibility and the horror.

On the surface, Eliot Nailles seems to be as lucky in the circumstances of his life as Paul Hammer was unlucky. Born, raised, and educated more conventionally than Hammer, he loves his wife, his son, his work, his house, Bullet Park, driving the volunteer fire truck, cutting wood with his chain saw. The opposition of their names signals some other contrasts between the protagonists. In addition to the marital and family happiness of Nailles in contrast to the lack of those things in Hammer's life, Nailles is also in touch with nature whereas Hammer isn't. Nailles loves the changes in the weather, fishing, and his aged hunting dog, Tessie, while Hammer, seeing the infirmity of the dog, suggests that she should be shot. Nailles seems to be an appreciative, creative participant in the world, while Hammer is the perennial outsider.

However, on closer scrutiny, we see certain limitations of character and vision in Nailles as well as some dark and violent impulses of his own. His limitations are primarily of perception; he is a simple man, thrown by complexity and suffering with which he has had little experience. We are told that "Nailles thought of pain and suffering as a principality lying somewhere beyond the legitimate borders of Western Europe. The government would be feudal and the country mountainous but it would never lie on his itinerary and would be unknown to his travel agent" (p. 50). We learn not only of this ignorance of darker sides to life, but of another sort of simplicity in Nailles: "One of Nailles' great liabilities was an inability to judge people on their appearance. He thought all men and women honest, reliable, clean and happy and he was often surprised and disappointed" (p. 53). In the novel, Tony's illness ends Nailles' inexperience with pain and grief, and in his attempt to deal with this blow, he is brought out of this state of prelapsarian innocence which has led him to believe simplistically in the goodness of all people, the predictability of life, and the solidity of the earth itself.

Furthermore, as Nailles moves away from the simple faith that has guided his life, certain parallels with Hammer emerge, much to our surprise. The compulsiveness of Hammer has a parallel in Nailles's suddenly one day being unable to complete his trip to the city on the commuter train. A doctor prescribes tranquillizers, and by the end of the novel, Nailles is dealing with a drug pusher in order to be able to get to his office. The seriousness of this sudden visitation of a phobia is that it undermines Nailles' sense of coherence and reason as governing the world. The fact that he develops a phobia about trains may be precipitated by the fact that he saw a neighbor fall or jump under the wheels of a train one day; but it is really the mysterious illness of his beloved son that destroys Nailles' sense of order and tranquillity. Thus Nailles, who seems at first the opposite of Hammer, comes to share with him a degree of irrational psychological behavior. Another more surprising link develops between the two. Hammer is finally the one who plans and almost succeeds in a murder. But throughout the novel it is Nailles who, on four different occasions, contemplates killing someone; and in three of the instances, the emotion is clearly murderous. The first time, embarrassed by the drunken antics of his father in front of a friend from Nailles school, he wishes his father dead. Another time — from humane motives — he contemplates killing his mother, who is lying unconscious after a stroke from which she will never recover. The third — and most serious — instance occurs when he quarrels with his son; the boy taunts him with the meaninglessness of his work, and Nailles strikes at him with a golf putter, missing splitting his skull only because Tony ducks and runs away. Lest we assume that this is only a threatening gesture, Cheever lets Nailles fill us in on his feelings:

"So there I was on this ruined miniature golf course having practically murdered my son but what I wanted to do then was to chase after him and take another crack at him with the putter. I was very angry. I couldn't understand how my only son, whom I love more than anything in the world, could make me want to kill him. (p. 118)

Far too simple to understand the psychological relationship of love and hate in the human psyche, Nailles is prey to angers that mystify him, the last manifestation of which occurs when Hammer suggests that Nailles shoot his dog. For a moment Nailles wants to murder Hammer. All of these reactions on Nailles' part lead us to see what seems to be Cheever's real intention in characterization in *Bullet Park*. Rather than intending his characters to be some sort of stick-figure opposites, the two men are closer to being alter egos. Murderous impulses may reside in any human heart, as we see that they do in the heart of Nailles; but Hammer, because of the insanity which renders him impervious to the restraining effects of society and human community, is the one who externalizes such impulses while Nailles does not. Hammer is an uncontrolled version of what most people, Nailles included, may have it in them to be at their worst moments. He is also — along with Tony's illness and his train phobia — a mysterious visitation in Nailles' life, the chance entrance into an orderly, happy life of violence and malevolence.

The plot level of the novel emphasizes chance, although it gives some occasional clues as to causality that in their inadequacy are almost more frustrating than would be the attribution of the events to blind chance. For instance, in racking his memory to think what could have caused Tony's refusal to get up, a refusal that could end in atrophy and death, Nailles remembers the night he threw the television set out of the house because Tony watched it too much, the day that Tony was pulled off the football team because of his low grades, and, of course, the fact that he had struck at him with a golf putter, an event that occurs the night before Tony's strange malady strikes. All of these events could add up to some explanation, but Tony himself brings up none of them, saying only that he feels sad. After doctors and psychologists have failed to cure him, Tony's parents call in a swami recommended to them by a former cleaning lady; the oddness of such an act underscores their desperation. Tony is healed in a matter of hours. The murder attempt on Tony is also handled in such a way as to emphasize the role of chance. Why Hammer chooses Tony as his victim after having settled upon Nailles to crucify as a typical suburbanite is never explained. Then Hammer inexplicably reveals his plan to the swami, who rushes to warn Nailles. Nailles arrives at Christ Church to find the doors locked and to hear Hammer say that he will burn Tony on the altar as soon as he finishes smoking a cigarette. Hammer's chance desire for a cigarette allows Nailles to rush home and get his chain saw and cut through the church door to rescue his son. The fact that both the choice of victim and the victim's salvation are so totally a matter of chance is the sobering truth that underlies this almost unbelievable series of events.

From this whole account, it should be clear that, despite some of the critics' complaints, Cheever was not writing just one more attack on suburbia. For the purposes of his real subject here, the suburb of *Bullet Park* provides a workable setting but is not itself the focus. The real subject is societal to this extent: the fact that Hammer plans and tries to carry out a murder while Nailles restrains his murderous impulses shows the value of society as a restraining force on our darkest possibilities. But the most important subject of the novel is the presence of good and evil or, perhaps in this novel, just evil. Evil is seen to be powerful; in *Bullet Park,* what goes wrong with the characters is a life-and-death matter rather than a function of country-club dances and high-salaried jobs. But worse, evil is also random, coming from nowhere, choosing its victims by chance, and leaving its mark. It is made more terrible by its appearance in a world where there is also a degree of love, order, and tranquillity. As John Gardner remarked: "What emerges here is a world where hope does exist (magic is real and can cure or kill), a world in a way even grimmer than Beckett's because here love and sacrifice are realities, like hope, but realities in flux, perpetually threatened, perishing."[11] In other words, a world depicted without love or hope is less tragically susceptible to the entrance of evil than a world populated by persons who try to sustain love and hope in their lives. Also, the novel deals through the portrayal of Nailles with the effects of an initiation into a knowledge of evil on a person previously unacquainted with it. While it is true that Nailles is allowed to save his son at the end of the novel, he would have done that anyway, on page one if that was when Tony was threatened. His love for his son is shown from the beginning to be so great that Tony's illness and near death cannot really increase it. And the last line of the novel makes clear how unredemptive the suffering of Nailles has been: "Tony went back to school on Monday and Nailles — drugged — went off to work and everything was as wonderful, wonderful, wonderful, wonderful as it had been" (p. 245). Readers are likely to be reminded, as the *Time* reviewer was, of the five bitter "nothings" in *King Lear* by this list of "wonderfuls." The repetition undercuts and finally erases the literal meaning of the word. Cheever refuses to suggest that Nailles is better off for his suffering or that he can be cured by taking up woodworking. What affirmation there is in the novel lies in the fact that a simple, optimistic man has been able to assimilate grief and suffering and an awareness of evil without being totally destroyed; it is the affirmation of survival rather than of transcendence.

It does not seem to me that the book has a serious problem with structure. The structure is very simple but neither "brokenbacked" nor overly episodic. Benjamin DeMott, in his criticism of the structure, was apparently troubled by the fact that Part One is devoted to Nailles, Part Two completely to Hammer, and Part Three, briefly, to the attempted murder. But Part One subtly prepares us for the importance of Hammer in the story; he figures in four chapters, despite the emphasis on Nailles. He is, in fact, the first person we meet in the novel, the man who comes to look at houses in Bullet Park in Chapter One. He appears at church; he invites the Nailleses to his house for dinner; he is on the train platform the day the man is killed. He is a significant enough figure in Part One that we are prepared for his centrality in Part Two and his role in the events of Part Three. Furthermore, the novel is episodic only in that the characters systematically think back over the past in order to understand the present. In Part One, Nailles tries to reconstruct the events of Tony's life for a clue as to the cause of his illness, but it is the illness itself which dominates Part One and unifies these reminiscences. In Part Two, Hammer's journal also reconstructs the formative events of his life, all with an eye to explaining how it can be that he is about to embark upon a premeditated murder. The novel has considerably more unity, in fact, than Cheever had previously achieved in the Wapshot novels.

Last, some critics charged that the style was inadequate to the subject matter, too lyrical or too light for such serious events and ideas. It seems to me that such a complaint overlooks the matter of voice, which is a particularly crucial and effective device in this novel. There is first of all the voice of the narrator, whose commentary on events stands quite apart from the judgments which Nailles and Hammer make on those same events. He is the one who sets the scene, rejects the narrow criticism of the adolescent in Chapter One, and tips us off to his final meaning by the use of too many "wonderfuls" in the final sentence of the novel. His distance, his judgments, and his irony, when he wishes it, are always clear. The undue lyricism that comes through in the novel is all a function of the viewpoint of Nailles, who *is* sentimental, lyrical about nature, his son, his wife, even his chain saw, but in an unimaginative way. And Part Two, Hammer's journal, is written in an entirely different voice, cold, matter-of-fact, with the logic of madness. This section possesses neither the reflective distance of the narrator nor the sentimental lyricism of Nailles; it is a controlled handling of point of view which underlines frighteningly the character of the person telling his own story. Cheever here is as completely in charge of point of view or voice as he has ever been in the novel form, although this is an area of consistent excellence in his short stories. Cheever has avoided the usual mode of the realistic novel with its emphasis on showing rather than telling the story and has relied, as Gardner says, on voice, "secret of the willing suspension of disbelief that normally carries the fantasy or tale."[12] This story is not finally a fantasy, and that fact adds to its horror, but it asks us to believe in events that strain our credulity. It is the assured voice of the author-narrator which convinces us to put aside our doubts and enter the dangerous world of *Bullet Park*.

CHAPTER 7

The Brightening Vision:
The World of Apples

LARRY Woiwode, a contemporary American fiction writer, paid John Cheever a graceful but peculiarly modern compliment growing out of the current penchant for having writers of reputation review the works of their contemporaries. Woiwode revealed that he had agreed to review *The World of Apples* for the *New York Times* in order to receive and be able to read the book in advance of its publication. His conclusion about the book, significant in the light of his enthusiasm for Cheever's work, is that *The World of Apples* is "...an extraordinary book, a transfiguring experience for the reader, and Cheever at his best. There is more flexibility, daring, diversity and vigor in this book than in any other of Cheever's (except perhaps *Bullet Park*), as though Cheever were growing progressively young."[1] I would be hard-pressed to find a basis for disagreement with this assessment, fulsome as it is; but the peculiar phenomenon of *The World of Apples* is that I would be equally pressed to explain exactly why I agree. The "flexibility, daring, diversity and vigor" are descriptive and demonstrable qualities of the volume, but a clue to the difficulty in delineating one's sense of these stories may be found in Woiwode's saying that it is "extraordinary" and a "transfiguring experience." The book is, as he says, extraordinary in relation to Cheever's previous work in the degree and nature of its inventiveness and in its stylistic achievement. Cheever's style, most often described as lyrical, has always figured in the impact of his works, but it is somehow different in this volume. One reviewer described it as "charged with tranquillity."[2] There is both a degree of understatement and a luminosity in these stories that sets them apart from earlier ones. But these observations are peculiarly difficult to demonstrate, and a large part of the stories' effect will, I believe,

117

depend on the reader's direct experience of them, hence, Woi-wode's emphasis on the *experience* they provide. The volume contains some very fine stories, particularly "The Fourth Alarm," "Percy," "Artemis, the Honest Well Digger," and "The World of Apples." However, none of them is better than the masterpieces which have already been singled out from earlier volumes. Some are more effectively structured than others, and they differ greatly from one another in subject and style. No particular theme seems to connect a significant number of stories in the collection, except that the first and the last provide some small sense of roundedness to the volume by dealing with the uses of memory. But, as a whole, the volume defies classification — and easy analysis, for the stories make a variety of demands on the reader.

The first story in the collection, "The Fourth Alarm," seems at first to be one more Cheever story about Sunday in suburbia. The narrator is drinking gin on a Sunday morning, the housekeeper is entertaining the children, and the wife is away. Gradually we discover that a severe upset has taken place in this home. The narrator's wife, Bertha, has left husband, children, and job as a junior high school teacher, to appear in New York in *Ozamanides,* a nude play in which she must perform or simulate sexual acts. The turning point of her life came, she believes, during the audition for the show as she recounts it to her husband:

There I sat naked in front of these strangers and I felt for the first time in my life that I'd found myself. I found myself in nakedness. I felt like a new woman, a better woman. To be naked and unashamed in front of strangers was one of the most exciting experiences I'd ever had. (p. 5)[3]

This aberration horrifies the narrator, who would probably gladly change places with any husband of a rebellious wife in any other Cheever story. His initial reaction is to ask for a divorce, which she sees no reason to consent to; and a divorce lawyer informs him that simulated carnality is not a precedent for divorce in New York State. Finally, he goes to see his wife in the play, which is confusing in its plot and general in its sexuality. The experience evokes in the narrator nostalgia for the innocent movie theaters of his youth and reminds him of his favorite movie, *The Fourth Alarm,* in which a horse-drawn fire wagon and its crew wins the day against the new-fangled fire engines. As he remembers how caught up he was in that movie, he sees Ozamanides writing an obscenity on his wife's buttocks, a juxtaposition that leads him to wonder if his wife has forgotten their shared past:

> Had nakedness — its thrill — annihilated her sense of nostalgia? ... It was her gift gracefully to carry the memory of some experience into another tense. Did she, mounted in public by a stranger, remember any of the places where we had made love? ... Should I stand up in the theater and shout for her to return, return, return in the name of love, humor and serenity? (p. 8)

The idea that the past can help us maintain our capacity for love, humor, and serenity — all major values in Cheever's work — is not new, but the suggestion that the Sixties fascination with public sexuality may be a way to expunge the past is. At the end of the story, the audience is urged by the cast to disrobe and come up on stage. Willing to reopen communication with his wife, the narrator undresses and heads for the stage, but refuses to leave his wallet and keys behind despite the cast's chanting "Put down your lendings!" He says, "None of it was irreplaceable, but to cast it off would seem to threaten my essence" (p. 9). He dresses and leaves; outside it is snowing and he remembers that he has snow tires on his car. He tells us, "This gave me a sense of security and accomplishment that would have disgusted Ozamanides and his naked court; but I seemed not to have exposed my inhibitions but to have hit on some marvelously practical and obdurate part of myself" (pp. 9–10). It is clear that Cheever is ultimately sympathetic to the narrator. The unintelligibility of the play, its and Bertha's emphasis on nudity and sexuality for their own sake, and a wife's desertion of her family all add up to criticism of her choice, whereas the narrator, in speaking for memory, speaks for one of Cheever's consistently upheld values. The story captures, for all its humor, the dislocation of values precipitated by the alleged sexual revolution of the 1960s. Cheever also makes it clear how the new morality connects to the old Puritanism by making Bertha and the cast doctrinaire about the morality of nudity; they are as bound to their system as any Puritan could be.

"Percy" is an example of the family chronicle which Cheever creates so well. The details of the family involved echo some of Cheever's own family reminiscences, particularly the one involving a cousin who was a piano prodigy. This story, like others in the book, is also somewhat concerned with memory — the narrator addresses the issue:

Reminiscence, along with the cheese boards and ugly pottery sometimes given to brides, seems to have a manifest destiny with the sea. Reminiscences are written on such a table as this, corrected, published, read, and then they begin their inevitable journey toward the bookshelves in those houses and cottages one rents for the summer.... Unpopularity is surely some part of this drifting toward salt water, but since the sea is our most universal symbol for memory, might there not be some mysterious affinity between these published recollections and the thunder of waves? (p. 35)

He then begins his own reminiscence, but his attitude toward his material is not very clear; the tone is almost pure chronicle. He introduces the family in question, mentioning the ancestors, including abolitionists, mediums, a cousin who starved herself to death in sympathy for the Armenian famine, and heroic drunks, and pointing out that although they lived in Athenian Boston, "the family seemed much closer to the hyperbole and rhetoric that stem from Wales, Dublin, and the various principalities of alcohol" (p. 36). The story's focus is on the narrator's Aunt Florence, who called herself Percy and smoked cigars, practices involving no sexual ambiguity but assumed because in her chosen career of famous painter, she realized that women were not likely to be taken seriously. She finds it hard to support herself doing portraits because she is too critical and has a tendency to paint defects of physiognomy or character as she sees them. She falls in love with an unsuccessful doctor, upon whom she dotes despite his incapacity for fidelity. In order to support them, she turns to painting sentimental magazine covers, a career at which she succeeds but which leaves her feeling thwarted as an artist. Her first son, Lovell, shows some musical talent, and she pushes him into the life of a piano prodigy as an outlet for her own frustrated artistic energies. Her second son, Beaufort, is born mentally retarded, a development associated in the family lore with Percy's discovery shortly before the son's birth of one of her husband's infidelities. One summer when Percy is in Europe, Lovell gets a job as an electrician, falls in love with an immigrant girl who doesn't know or care that he plays the piano, and marries her, leading to a permanent estrangement from his mother. He dies young, and his mother dies soon afterwards, refusing to see a doctor for her ailment. The story ends with the narrator encountering Beaufort working as a janitor in an airport. He hurries away to catch his plane, and the story ends "And so off to the sea'' (p. 50). The matter-of-factness of this ending emphasizes the fact that this has been primarily a recollection of these characters; the narrator's attitude is not made clear, and no thematic point emerges from the reminiscence. The point seems to be portraiture pure and simple, and the story is a highly controlled piece of writing compared to some of Cheever's other efforts in this vein.

"Artemis, the Honest Well Digger" resembles both "The Fourth Alarm" and "Percy" in some ways. Like the former, it captures certain aspects of American cultural history in the 1960s. Like the latter, it also provides a detailed character sketch of its protagonist. Artemis is a well-driller who is poetic in his love for water in all its forms and in devotion to his craft. The tone and to some extent the story itself are prefigured in the following lines of introduction: "His father had chosen his name, thinking that it referred to artesian wells. It wasn't until Artemis was a grown man that he discovered that he had been named for the chaste goddess of the hunt. He didn't seem to mind and, anyhow, everybody called him Art" (p. 54). Though he is well educated and a voracious reader, he pretends to be rustic, feeling that this is the demeanor expected of well-drillers. His chastity is hinted at in the fact that despite having proposed marriage to several girls, he is still single at the age of thirty. One day while he is drilling, a woman insists he come in for coffee; she tells him that her husband — who is away — is a famous author who has written a book called *Shit*. She explains that

. . . he wanted to write a book about something that concerned everybody, like sex, only by the time he got his grant, everything you could write about sex had been written. Then he got this other idea. After all, it was universal. (p. 59)

Artemis reads the book and is surprised to find that the title is in no way metaphoric; he cannot believe that he lives in a world where a man could become famous for such a dubious accomplishment. Meanwhile, the woman falls in love with Artemis, and he decides to leave town until her infatuation passes. A travel agent talks him into going to Russia where he promptly falls in love with a translator; after one night with her, he is expelled from the country. They correspond in poetic, emotional letters until he is summoned to Washington, where State Department officials accuse him and Natasha of corresponding in code to pass vital information. The evidence of their spying is a hilarious piece of paranoid projection; the official summarizes the case:

> ...She wrote that God might sit in a submarine, surrounded by divisions of mermaids. That same day was the date of our last submarine crisis.... Earlier she wrote that you and she were a wave on the Black Sea. The date corresponds precisely to the Black Sea maneuvers. You sent her a photograph of yourself beside the Wakusha Reservoir, pointing out that this was the center of the Northeast watershed. This, of course, is not classified information, but it all helps. Later you write that the dark seems to you like a house divided into seventy rooms. This was written ten days before we activated the Seventieth Division. (p. 83)

Actually, all the couple is guilty of is preposterous epistolary style; but the official wants Artemis to plant false and misleading information in his next letters. He refuses, continues to write to her, but never hears from her again. "When it got warmer, there was the healing sound of rain to hear, at least there was that" (p. 84). On this elegiac note, the narrative ends. Despite the comedy and satire in the story, its dominant note is the poignant characterization of Artemis, a sort of portraiture at which Cheever excels.

The last story in the volume, "The World of Apples," is an interesting attempt to synthesize American and Italian cultures. Asa Bascomb is an aged famous poet, originally from Vermont, who has lived most of his adult life in Italy for reasons he cannot quite recall, either to give color to his stern New England outlook or to evade the publicity and interruptions that would have been more bothersome to an artist in America. He is famous primarily for one volume of poems, *The World of Apples,* a celebration of the beauties and possibilities of life. In the opening paragraphs of the story, he is swatting flies in his work house and wondering why he has not been awarded the Nobel Prize. That his question is not arrogant is attested to by the facts that he has received every other literary honor and that he is apparently a fine poet. In addition to producing work of high quality, he seems to possess a strength of character which sets him apart from his contemporaries; the four poets with which his work has been grouped all committed suicide. Bascomb had known, loved, and, in one case, nursed these colleagues, "but the broad implication that he had, by choosing to write poetry, chosen to destroy himself was something he rebelled against vigorously" (p. 162). Bascomb, in his eighties, is rendered vulnerable by his increasing loss of memory — and hence, he believes, his source of poetic power — and his regrets about the Nobel Prize. One day he comes upon a couple making love in the woods, and from this moment, he is obsessed by a pornographic demon; obscene thoughts suddenly seem to have more vitality and beauty than the world he has created in his work. In the next days, he writes an assortment of disgusting and vulgar sexual memoirs, scatalogical epic poems, dirty limericks. During these days he is frequently interrupted by nuns, innocent couples, and fresh-faced youths who come to pay their respects and ask him to autograph their copies of *The World of Apples,* a juxtaposition which adds to his feeling of guilt and uncleanness. Finally one day he can do nothing but write "Fuck" over and over on numerous sheets of paper. His housekeeper, unaware of his plight, mentions that in the church at Monte Giordano, there is a sacred angel who can cleanse thoughts. Feeling like a fool, Bascomb sets out on a pilgrimage. He offers the angel the gold medal presented him by the Soviet government and prays, "God bless Walt Whitman. God bless Hart Crane. God bless Dylan Thomas. God bless William Faulkner, Scott Fitzgerald, and especially Ernest Hemingway" (p. 173). Despite the fact that many of these writers were self-destructive where he has been strong, this litany apparently reestablishes Bascomb's sense of solidarity with them and his own best and creative self, and that night he sleeps peacefully again, untroubled by dreams of perverse sensuality. On the way home, Bascomb comes upon a waterfall, the sound of which evokes one of his important childhood memories. Sitting on a ledge above a waterfall in the Vermont woods near his home:

... he saw an old man, with hair as thick and white as his was now, come through the woods. He had watched the old man unlace his shoes and undress himself with the haste of a lover. First he had wet his hands and arms and shoulders and then he had stepped into the torrent, bellowing with joy. He had then dried himself with his underpants, dressed, and gone back into the woods and it was not until he disappeared that Bascomb had realized that the old man was his father. (p. 174)

Now Bascomb does the same thing. After a minute he can no longer stand the cold, "but when he stepped away from the water he seemed at last to be himself" (p. 174). This baptism or Hemingway-type purification by nature now restores him to his own past, just as the prayer in the church restored him to his literary tradition. He returns home. "In the morning he began a long poem on the inalienable dignity of light and air that, while it would not get him the Nobel Prize, would grace the last months of his life'' (p. 174). This may be the best story in the volume — carefully imagined, effectively paced, beautifully expressed. It is also tempting to see it as a quiet manifesto on Cheever's part. Always before the title story of a volume has been first, but here this one may have been placed last so as to leave us with the memory of the artist who does not feel that it is necessary to self-destruct, who, though sympathetic to those who break apart because of their view of the world, has the personal courage to survive and the artistic courage, in our age, to try to render the subjects of light and air in *their* dignity. Asa Bascomb, decades his senior, seems a version of Cheever — a writer who by valuing the past and honoring the best in literary tradition and celebrating the light and air has himself avoided the temptations of suicide and confronted in art the sustaining forces of life.

Two other stories in the collection deserve mention, one because it is an odd sort of failure and the other because it is in the mold of Cheever's most successful mysterious stories. The first, "The Jewels of the Cabots," is set in St. Botolphs and reworks some of the material that was in the background of the Wapshot novels; but it seems to me that every time after *The Wapshot Chronicle* that Cheever returns to this material, the result is more disjointed and less satisfying artistically than before. *The Wapshot Scandal* was more disorganized than the first Wapshot novel, and this story seems never to decide what its purpose and point are. Is it primarily the narrator's reflections upon St. Botolphs and its contrast to his present life written in the style of Coverly Wapshot? (At one point the unnamed narrator says his father is Leander, but nothing else identifies him as a Wapshot; he more resembles the detached narrator of *The Wapshot Scandal*.) Perhaps the primary point is simply the story of the Cabots, almost Gothic in its inclusion of a secret encephalitic child, diamonds stolen by a daughter who runs away from home, a mistress and illegitimate child on the poor side of town, and the arsenic poisoning of Mr. Cabot by his wife which everyone suspects but no one is willing to pursue. Is the purpose to distinguish the genteel West Bank life of St. Botolphs from the East Side where the tenements and factories are? If so, the point is not clear since the jewel theft and the poisoning take place on the elite West Bank. Is the story primarily interested in depicting New England eccentricity, such as Mrs. Cabot's hanging her diamonds to dry on the clothesline once a week? All of this and more goes on in the story, and the movement between elements is jerky; and, despite some good scenes, the final meaning is unclear.

"The Geometry of Love," on the other hand, is a weirdly mysterious story, like "The Enormous Radio" or "The Music Teacher," in which some sort of magic seems to have real efficacy rather than being a figment of a character's imagination. Charlie Mallory, an engineer, discovers a way to use geometry to deal with difficulties in his life. He finds that if he can translate trouble with his wife or business tensions into geometric terms, he can take away their ability to hurt and worry him.

> As he continued with his study and his practice, he discovered that the rudeness of headwaiters, the damp souls of clerks, and the scurrilities of traffic policemen could not touch his tranquillity, and that these oppressors, in turn, sensing his strength, were less rude, damp, and scurrilous.... He thought of writing a book about his discovery: *Euclidean Emotion: The Geometry of Sentiment.* (p. 148)

He even finds, on a business trip to Chicago, that he can render the gloom of Gary, Indiana, less affecting; on a later trip, however, he miscalculates, and Gary disappears altogether. Sometime later, Mallory is taken seriously ill. During his convalescence, his unsympathetic wife visits and upsets him, and he realizes that he will have to use geometry in order to avoid a relapse. Remembering, however, what happened to Gary, Indiana, he proceeds very cautiously with his calculations. Something goes wrong, nevertheless; and when his wife gets home, she learns that he has died. This story is primarily an entertainment, a fabulous account of the dangers of applying scientific principles too effectively to the human world. At first the story seems humorous and Mallory a mild eccentric; only gradually do we realize that the power of geometry is taking over, much as radios and piano exercises did in other Cheever stories of this kind.

In "The Jewels of the Cabots," there is a passage that serves as a gloss not only on the triumphant restoration of Asa Bascomb in the title story of this volume but also on the ideas of most of the other stories. The narrator says:

> Children drown, beautiful women are mangled in automobile accidents, cruise ships founder, and men die lingering deaths in mines and submarines, but you will find none of this in my accounts. In the last chapter the ship comes home to port, the children are saved, the miners will be res-

cued. Is this an infirmity of the genteel or a conviction that there are discernible moral truths? Mr. X defecated in his wife's top drawer. This is a fact, but I claim that it is not a truth. (p. 24)

Cheever has never been simply a chronicler of manners, a photographer of cultural artifacts; but in this volume, more than any other, he seems anxious to make this clear distinction between *fact* and *truth*. He has always tried to get to the motives and morality of his characters which underlie the manners and material aspects of their lives, but in this collection particularly, the human truths involved seem to transcend the factual circumstances of the stories. Perhaps this is what Woiwode meant when he said the book is a "transfiguring experience," in which case his words are not fulsome praise but an analytical attempt to express the purpose and the method of Cheever's accomplishment in these stories.

CHAPTER 8

Falconer: *A Dramatic Departure for Familiar Territory*

THE astonishment on the part of Cheever's readers and *aficionados* which greeted the publication of *Falconer* (1977) is not difficult to understand if one reads only the opening sentences of the novel:

> The main entrance to Falconer — the only entrance for convicts, their visitors and the staff — was crowned by an escutcheon representing Liberty, Justice and, between the two, the sovereign power of government.... How many hundreds had passed under this, the last emblem most of them would see of man's endeavor to interpret the mystery of imprisonment in terms of symbols.... Above the escutcheon was a declension of the place names: Falconer Jail 1871, Falconer Reformatory, Falconer Federal Penitentiary, Falconer State Prison, Falconer Correctional Facility, and the last, which had never caught on: Daybreak House. Now cons were inmates, the assholes were officers and the warden was a superintendent. (p. 3)[1]

Cheever, the chronicler of large cities, affluent suburbs, and charming New England villages, has set his latest novel in a prison? When has he ever before been concerned with Liberty or Justice as capitalized concepts, much less the "sovereign power of government"? The time the last appeared in a Cheever work, it came in the form of the IRS in *The Wapshot Scandal;* and its sovereignty had been easily thwarted by Honora's quixotic suicide. When has this genteel writer ever used language like "asshole"? What is going on here?

The second paragraph is not reassuring. We learn that the protagonist of this novel is indeed a prisoner "Farragut (fratricide, zip to ten, #734-508-32)." We have been aware of fraternal tensions in Cheever's previous work, but now for the first time we have an actual murder. Worse, we discover that the hero is not only a murderer but a heroin addict on a methadone maintenance regimen. Anything that future pages reveal about Ezekiel Farragut's background — involving the more familiar Cheever territory of suburban life and a white-collar profession, complicated by family eccentricities and marital discontinuities — is more than offset by our awareness of Farragut's fratricide, drug addiction, and vivid experiences as a prisoner in Falconer, including a homosexual love affair, something else unprecedented in Cheever's work. No work of Cheever's has departed so dramatically from the terrain — both geographical and psychological — of his previous books. One can see some continuity from earlier works in the subject and values of this novel, but the use of Falconer Prison as the crucible in which this protagonist will be tried and tested is a shocking and radical change of direction for Cheever. It almost seems as if Cheever had read — and decided to respond in fiction to — this remark which John Aldridge made about his career:

He still needs to find something more and, above all, different to say about his subject.... He needs to break out of his present mode and rearrange or retool his imaginative responses, not only so that he will be able to confront squarely the full implications of his vision, but so that his vision can become in fact a vision.... One wishes to say to him what Gertrude Stein once said to Hemingway: begin over again and concentrate. For he does not yet disturb us enough. He does not yet rouse enough fear.[2]

One doesn't have to agree fully with the assumptions underlying Aldridge's remark to appreciate how, deliberately or not, Cheever has answered it in *Falconer*. He *has* broken out of every mode we have ever seen him use. By locating the values that inform all his fiction in the unpromising setting of a prison, he makes us believe, more than ever, in the profound and tested constancy with which he holds to his vision of the world. He has written a book that does indeed disturb and frighten, but a book that finally allows his values and vision to triumph more definitively than ever before in his work.

It is predictable that reviewers and readers would have scanned Cheever's recent years for some clue in his personal life to explain this surprising change of fictional direction. Some have found some possible explanation in two cataclysmic events which preceded the writing of the novel — a near-fatal heart attack at age sixty which necessitated hospitalization and restricted activity and then a serious bout with alcoholism which led to a period of confinement in a recovery center. People have also noted that his teaching writing at Sing Sing in his home town of Ossining may have given him not only the details of a prison setting but an emotional grasp of the psychology of incarceration. Cheever tends to discount this last element, saying in one interview that he did no conscious research during his teaching stint at the prison and in another that his "only first-hand experience with confinement had been in stuck elevators, fogged-in airports, and mistaken erotic contacts."[3] It is, of course, possible that some of Cheever's interest in and comprehension of the effects of imprisonment do proceed from his own experiences of enforced confinement in these years as well as from the sense of being trapped that can come in everyday occurrences; but at least as important would be the relationship between his recovery from a heart attack and alcoholism and the triumphant affirmation of *Falconer* — less qualified than in any other book. His daughter remarked while interviewing him that his family and friends felt he had returned from the dead when he came home from the recovery center. Walter Clemons associates the affirmation of the novel with Cheever's escape from his "descent toward death" and calls *Falconer* "the triumphant work of a man newborn."[4] And R. Z. Sheppard noting the absence of vengefulness in Farragut at the novel's end, the point of which seems to be that "survival is always a miracle and reward enough," concludes insightfully: "*Falconer* is not a young man's book."[5] Just as Cheever's affirmation in *Falconer* reverberates more loudly for emerging from a painful prison experience rather than from a comfortable suburban existence, so he may have felt a greater urgency to let life-enhancing values triumph after having himself come so close to the brink of death.

The most obvious departure from his earlier work in *Falconer* is, of course, the setting, which involves not only the physical locale but the characters who populate the prison, very unlike the denizens of Cheever's usual urbane world. The setting is captured in a few precise details, such as the bars of the cells, once painted white but now worn black at chest height where the prisoners instinctively grip them. The general disrepair and soul-destroying shabbiness of a large state prison is revealed in the description of the toilet in Farragut's cell, which flushes of its own accord and lets him get very few nights of uninterrupted sleep. Cheever has gone to some lengths to create a vividly different human setting as well, by placing Farragut, despite his prestigious background and upperclass accent, not in cellblock A, with the lieutenant governor, the secretary of commerce, and the millionaires, but in F, where he is surrounded by a variety of criminals all known to us by nicknames. Tennis was a minor tennis champion in prison for forgery, referred to by him as "a clerical error"; Chicken Number Two claims to have been a brilliant jewel thief but talks in his sleep in the slang of a pimp; the Cuckold, given to loquacious recitals of his marital difficulties, killed his wife "by mistake"; Bumpo is the second man ever to have hijacked an airplane; Stone had his eardrums pierced and was set up for arrest by the syndicate; Ransome's crime is not mentioned but his tender watchfulness over the helpless Stone is. The other important character in the cellblock is Tiny, an obese guard, who is responsible for a stomach-curdling massacre of the prison cats, but who is otherwise gentle and solicitous of the prisoners, especially of Farragut, whose addiction puzzles and upsets him. Cheever also captures the manners that govern prison life from the delicacy that prevents the prisoners from asking questions of each other about their crimes to the existence of the Valley, a urinal trough where the men line up to masturbate but even here according to strict rules that insure a degree of courtesy. He catches the bureaucratese that marks communication but which sometimes trails off into the vernacular as in the following memo:

LOUISA PIERCE SPINGARN, IN MEMORY OF HER BELOVED SON PETER, HAS ARRANGED FOR INTERESTED INMATES TO BE PHOTOGRAPHED IN FULL COLOR BESIDE A DECORATED CHRISTMAS TREE AND TO HAVE SAID PHOTOGRAPHS MAILED AT NO COST TO THE INMATE'S LOVED ONES. PICTURE-TAKING WILL BEGIN AT 900/8/27 IN THE ORDER OF RECEIVED APPLICATIONS. WHITE SHIRTS ALLOWABLE. DON'T BRING NOTHING BUT A HANDKERCHIEF. (p. 145)

In his use of the prison setting, Cheever brings out many facts of prison life — bullying officials who deliberately skip Farragut's methadone fix and watch his withdrawal agonies for entertainment, poignant visits across a table separated by wire mesh, a radio report of the Attica riot followed by nervous restrictive measures in other prisons; but he avoids some of the worst known aspects of prison life, such as homosexual rape, contraband smuggling, and racial violence, so as to concentrate on the effects of incarceration on the human spirit of an unlikely prisoner like Farragut and his attempts to survive.

The second most obvious departure in this novel involves Cheever's diction. There are still passages of lyrical celebration — of nature, sunlight, and remembered love — mostly in Farragut's reflections or in letters; and there are some philosophical musings on the essence of things, also reminiscent of Cheever's more familiar prose style. But *Falconer* is full of obscene and profane language, both in the characters' dialogue and in the narrative itself. As John Leonard observed, the characters "don't sound like Coverly Wapshot."[6] The word "asshole" seems to appear on every page of the novel, sometimes in reference to the guards, sometimes to the prisoners, sometimes to the weather. The effect is similar to that of the repeated "so it goes" in Vonnegut's *Slaughterhouse Five;* it sensitizes the reader to the underlying point, which in the case of *Falconer* is the powerlessness of the men which leaves them only the weaponry of profanity. In another departure from Cheever's usually genteel style, every vernacular term for genitalia and sexual intercourse appears, most of them repeatedly. Cheever has always included the fact of human carnality in his fiction, but he has treated it lyrically and with celebration for the most part. Here he is downright clinical, and this development has shocked some of his readers. Part of the point of this surprising use of language may be to deal frankly with the sexual problems of imprisoned men and their inability to fulfill their needs except through homosexual encounters, masturbation, and lurid fantasies about their sexual encounters on the outside.

One of the biggest surprises for a reader familiar with Cheever's previous work is the attitude he takes here toward homosexuality. Homosexuality has been mentioned minimally in Cheever work's before; and while it has never been denounced, it has usually been regretted and rejected by Cheever's protagonists. Coverly Wapshot, for instance, is thrown into an emotional tailspin in *The Wapshot Chronicle* by the suspicion that he may be homosexual engendered by a superior at work making a pass at him. His unfounded anxiety serves to demonstrate his naiveté and his heterosexuality and to dismiss the idea of homosexuality from a range of acceptable sexual behavior. And the only clearly drawn homosexual in Cheever's previous work, Mr. Rowantree in "Clancy in the Tower of Babel," is treated stereotypically. In *Falconer* for the first time

Cheever allows for a tender love relationship between two men. Farragut has been an avid pursuer and romancer of women, and he is as surprised as the reader when he discovers that he has fallen in love with Jody, a seductive younger man who is no more a committed homosexual than Farragut but who has adapted himself to this sexual option of imprisoned men. But Cheever's point in including homosexuality in his novel becomes clear in his treatment of this relationship; he does not dwell on its physical consummation but its emotional import, as in the way Farragut finds himself listening for the footsteps of his lover. Also, in the scene in which they meet, it becomes clear that besides love, Jody has a wonderful hideout to offer Farragut, a place in the catwalk where they have a view of the river and the hills beyond the prison walls, something as important to Farragut as sexual satisfaction. The point of including this experience seems to be to expand Farragut's notions of what love is — and even here not so much that it can be extended to partners of one's own gender as that it can be emotionally sustaining without being possessive. When Jody plans to escape, Farragut wishes only for his safety; when news comes that he is married, Farragut wishes only for his happiness.

Another phenomenon which has not appeared in Cheever's work to the degree that it does in *Falconer* is violence. To be sure, violent events do occur in his earlier work. A number of suicides take place. Cash Bentley is shot by his wife in "O Youth and Beauty," and Hammer tries to immolate Nailles's son in *Bullet Park*. But these acts usually take place offstage and are neither described nor elaborated upon. But in *Falconer,* the emotional violence in Farragut's wife's visits, the psychic violence to the men's dignity by demeaning physical examinations and total loss of privacy, and the potential violence hovering on the edge of the novel if the riot should spread from Attica to Falconer Prison color the mood. In addition, an act of violence has sent Farragut to prison in the first place and a nauseating massacre of prison cats occurs after two of them steal the guard's dinner. This last violent episode has a particularly great influence on the inmates, many of whom have pets to assuage their loneliness; they smuggle food to them, and some convicts risk solitary confinement rather than turn over their particular favorites for the guards to kill. This scene seems to function in the novel not so much to disgust and shock the reader as to convey the degree of the men's loneliness and also to introduce a religious element into Farragut's behavior. The scene ends with him praying, an action which, in its occurring outside church walls, is unusual in Cheever's fiction.

Religion has always figured in Cheever's fiction but mostly as a matter of manners. A number of Cheever's heroes — Coverly Wapshot, Johnny Hake, Eliot Nailles — are regular communicants in Episcopal churches. There is, John Leonard says, a kind of "muscular Episcopalianism"[7] in Cheever's work, but its day-to-day meaning in characters' lives has never been explored in any depth and its expression is almost always limited to institutional church ritual. In *Falconer,* the religious content is direct, overt, and pervasive. Early in the novel Farragut writes a lengthy letter to his bishop in which he states his religious stance:

...to profess religious experience outside the ecclesiastical paradigm is to make of oneself an outcast.... I truly believe in One God the Father Almighty but I know that to say so loudly, and at any distance from the chancel — any distance at all — would dangerously jeopardize my ability to ingratiate those men and women with whom I wish to live. I am trying to say that while we are available to transcendent experience, we can state this only at the suitable and ordained time and in the suitable and ordained place. I could not live without this knowledge; no more could I live without the thrilling possibility of suddenly encountering the fragrance of skepticism. (p. 72)

Farragut, now in a place with no "suitable and ordained" forms of religious expression, will have to move beyond this view; in the course of the novel he comes to integrate his religious impulses into his ongoing daily life. For one thing, he prays on several occasions, not ritual prayers — though he relies on the ritual words — but deeply personal expressions torn out of him at moments of crisis. After the massacre of the cats, he can only kneel in his bunk and murmur, "Blessed are the meek," and after he succeeds in building a secret radio during the Attica riot, he hears himself mumbling "Praise be to thee, O Lord." Deprived of the opportunity for ritual worship, he finds himself worshiping quietly in his daily life. In fact, during a flu epidemic, a young priest wanders into his cell and gives him the Holy Eucharist; afterwards, Farragut is almost irritated by the intrusion of this familiar form into his new life.

But the most important aspect of Cheever's use of religion in *Falconer* involves his use of the religious paradigm to illuminate Farragut's experience. Prepared for by nomenclature — Ezekiel means "God strengthens" — the novel traces in Farragut's experience a fall, trial, and redemption pattern. His fall is, of course, the murder of his brother and the self-destructiveness of his drug addiction. His trial is to survive with some sense of himself the alienating experience of imprisonment and indeed to fnd new aspects of humanity in himself and his fellow inmates. The quality of his love for Jody and the assimilation of religious impulses and expressions into his whole life prepare him for redemption. But he really has to *earn* his right to escape, which he does when he takes the dying Chicken Number Two into his own cell to care for during the flu epidemic and — in a Christly gesture — washes the suffering man before making him comfortable in his own bed. That night Chicken dies, and in a moment of clarity in his grief, Farragut sees his chance to take the dead man's place in the bag in which his body will be removed for burial without ceremony as a NKRC (No Known Relatives or Concerned). In previous Cheever works, the protagonists have been saved in the end — Johnny Hake from a life of crime, Tony Nailles from Hammer's planned sacrificial immolation, Blake from the woman with a gun on the commuter train — but notably *not* through their own efforts or desserts. Here, in another departure, Farragut is made to undergo a period of testing and trial and has to perform an act symbolic of his new deservingness of salvation. The only improvement in his life for which he cannot take credit is his shaking off of his drug addiction; he has been gradually reduced in methadone dosage, then given placebos, and one day he suddenly learns that he is clean. This is not a state for which he has struggled but perhaps a reward prior to his escape; certainly it makes his chance of survival on the outside better. There is no question that the resurrection image informs Farragut's escape; by the agency of Chicken's death and in Chicken's shroud, feigning death himself, he escapes to new life. He slits the bag while the guards are occupied, incurring some razor wounds in the process. He is befriended by a stranger, who in another biblical parallel gives him an extra coat to cover his bloody prison garb. After making his escape and experiencing the brotherly charity of the stranger, Farragut sets off down the street head high, back straight, not so much restored as reborn into the world. The novel's last line emphasizes the triumph of the religious attitude which has pervaded this novel: "Rejoice, he thought, rejoice" (p. 211). In a passage in the letter to his bishop — which seemed self-serving at the time in the novel at which Farragut wrote it — he says that as a prisoner my life follows very closely the traditional lives of the saints.... We prisoners, more than any men, have suffered for our sins, we have suffered for the sins of society, and our example should cleanse the thoughts of men's hearts because of the grief with which we are acquainted. (pp. 72–73)

By the end of *Falconer* we realize that the meaning of the novel is prefigured in that passage: that there is a saintliness, a Christlike capacity in Farragut to which he is brought by the suffering of the prison situation and his own attempt to find meaning and transcendence within it.

This very religious focus on a man's moving through trial to redemption is aided by a technical departure in the novel. *Falconer* is one of very few works in which Cheever uses limited third-person point of view. Except for one scene — the escape of Jody aided by an archbishop in an echo of *Les Miserables* — the entire story is filtered through the consciousness of Farragut. For this novel, Cheever has given up his customarily pronounced use of an authorial narrator who comments intrusively and at length on the meaning of the events. His decision is well taken. As one reviewer noted, this much focus on a single character is altogether new in Cheever's work.[8] But in this story, since the character is to undergo radical internal changes, it is crucial that we be let in on his consciousness of what he is going through. For the novel to achieve its religious meaning, it is important that we understand not only Farragut's behavior but the workings of his soul. All of the elements which seem so different from Cheever's usual practice — prison setting, convicts as characters, crude language, violence in the surroundings, an understanding attitude toward drugs and homosexuality, and the narrative viewpoint of a center of consciousness — work to underscore the greatest difference of all of this novel from Cheever's earlier work — the degree of direct religious affirmation it expresses.

At the same time there are some continuities between Cheever's earlier work and *Falconer*. It is important to note them because their presence emphasizes the author's willingness to integrate the affirmation in *Falconer* — unqualified by wryness, irony, or fortuitousness — with the materials of his whole career. Most of these continuities involve Ezekiel Farragut himself; his life and experiences echo those of other Cheever characters. Like many Cheever characters, he lives in a suburb, though one never before used in the

author's geography, Indian Hill, Southwick, Connecticut. He is the
first academic, a college professor, since the narrator of "Goodby,
My Brother." Nothing much is made of his career except that his
white-collar background distinguishes him from the other inmates
of Cellblock F: it also gives him additional emotional and linguistic
resources with which to deal with his incarceration. The main
echoes of previous characters in Farragut's life involve his parents,
who are like the Wapshots to some degree, his troubled relationship
with his brother, Eben, and his relatively unhappy marriage.

Farragut's parents are reminiscent of Leander and Sarah Wapshot, though much less sympathetic and given to us in much less
detail. His father, like Leander, teaches his son to fish and to appreciate nature but otherwise neglects him, spending most of his time
sailing a little catboat around Travertine Harbor, a town name
readers will recall from the Wapshot novels. Unlike Leander, he is
given to self-pity and suicide threats. Farragut's most vivid memory
dates back to his sixteenth year when he sees his father threatening
to jump off a roller-coaster at Nagakasit (to which Leander piloted
his ferry) and entertaining the crowd with his clownish antics.
Farragut gets him down, saying, "Oh, Daddy, . . . you shouldn't
do this to me in my formative years" (p. 62). Mrs. Farragut is like
Sarah Wapshot — none too sympathetic to her husband, fiercely
independent, and a self-sufficient business woman. The family's
eccentricity is summed up in this line: "The Farraguts were the sort
of people who claimed to be sustained by tradition, but who were in
fact sustained by the much more robust pursuit of a workable
improvisation, uninhibited by consistency" (p. 59). It may be this
resilient part of his heritage that helps Farragut survive the experience of imprisonment. There is also a similar skeleton in the
family closet; like Leander, Farragut's father had wanted his second son aborted; in both cases, the reluctant fathers have gone so
far as to bring abortionists to their houses. In *The Wapshot
Chronicle,* Sarah takes pleasure in telling Coverly this story herself;
in *Falconer,* Eben conveys this information to Ezekiel during a
quarrel, leading the latter to strike his brother fatally with a
fireplace iron.

Relationships between brothers, often tense in Cheever, are at an
all-time low in *Falconer.* The clearest antecedent for this story is
"Goodby, My Brother." The relationship there is between a life-
celebrating narrator like Farragut and a gloomy doom-monger like
Eben, and an argument between the two results in the narrator's

hitting his brother in a moment of anger. The situation is the same in *Falconer,* except the consequences are fatal. The unusual aspect of the Farragut brothers is that Eben's hostility is so great that *he* has apparently tried to kill Ezekiel on at least two occasions, once by encouraging him to swim in an area where there is a dangerous undertow and once by pushing him out a window at a party. The novel doesn't really explain Eben's hatefulness, and it does show Ezekiel's attempts to overlook these lethal clues to his brother's hostility and hence to maintain some communication with him. In fact, were they totally estranged, Ezekiel would not have been present on the day of the fatal fight. Eben's general human destructiveness is attested to by his desperately unhappy wife and the ruined lives of his children. A possible reason for it may be that, like Richard in ''The Lowboy,'' Eben has gathered about him the furniture of his early family life and has ''quite unselfconsciously, reconstructed the environment of what he claimed was his miserable youth'' (p. 95). Perhaps, like Richard, his continuing to play out old angers and rivalries from his childhood explains the malevolence of his attitude toward his brother. In any event, the brothers quarrel, and Eben yells that their father wanted Ezekiel aborted, screaming, ''He loved me, but he wanted you to be killed'' (p. 198). Farragut strikes him with a fireplace tool. Obviously, this is an unpremeditated act, but the book is unclear as to the extent of Ezekiel's violence. The widow testifies at the trial that Ezekiel struck his brother eighteen or twenty times; Farragut claims that he hit him once, and Eben, drunk, hit his head on the stone hearth. There is no way to be sure, but certainly Farragut's unwillingness to admit to murder at the least underscores the seriousness of his attempts to maintain some sense of a fraternal bond. One does get the feeling that the suppressed violence of many fraternal relationships in Cheever's work has built up for years to this act of Farragut's, which cannot be called back and which changes his life, ultimately for the best, since his actual imprisonment frees him from the confinements of drugs, the past, and a bad marriage.

Just as the hostility in brotherly relationships in Cheever erupts in *Falconer,* so is Marcia, Farragut's wife, the culmination of all the unloving, destructive women in Cheever's fiction. All the frustrated women who take their discontent, legitimate or not, out on their husbands seem to have been pointing to the conception of Marcia. She is cruel rather than comforting in her only two visits to Farragut in prison, pointing out that she's been in Jamaica, refus-

ing to let him see his son on the advice of psychologists, pretending
to have lost a letter from the boy, and indicating no real interest but
a little salacious curiosity about his life by asking if he's been the
target of homosexual advances. She taunts him for his drug addiction and charges him with ruining her life. When Farragut, looking
for a neutral subject of conversation, asks about the house, she
replies: "Well, it's nice to have a dry toilet seat" (p. 28). Some of
her bitterness might be understandable in relation to the dislocation
caused in her life by her husband's crime and conviction, but we
learn that she has behaved similarly during most of their life together. She is the most narcissistic of Cheever heroines. An authen-
ticated beauty, the effect of her emotionally being one is devastating. Even her young son realizes that it is impossible to talk to her if
there is a mirror in the room, and she — at a moment propitious for
lovemaking — often stands before the bedroom mirror and asks,
"Is there another woman of my age in this county who is as beautiful as I?" (p. 18). She is the coldest, least sympathetic heroine in
Cheever's fiction, and Cheever does virtually nothing to explain or
justify her behavior. Her main function in the novel seems to be to
serve as part of Farragut's problem — a wife like her makes heroin
addiction plausible. Also, since her visits provide occasions for him
to deal with her forgivingly, they help precipitate his gradual salvation.
In any event, the portrait of Marcia Farragut is not likely to make people forget that Cheever's fiction contains a number of destructive, unlikable women or to quell the suspicion that he is at least something
of a male chauvinist.

   One more element that links Farragut to previous characters and
values in Cheever's work is his sensitivity to and love of nature. All
of Cheever's male protagonists in the novels — Leander, Moses
and Coverly, Nailles — are distinguished by the degree to which
they are at home in nature and to which they are sustained by it.
Farragut feels wrenched away from the world of blue skies as he
enters prison; his days can be changed for the better if the sunlight
falls in a certain slant through the window of his cell; and he gets
great pleasure from mowing the prison yard. Fall leaves dropping
in the yard remind him of the deep pleasure which he has always
taken in nature:

He liked to walk on the earth, swim in the oceans, climb the mountains
and, in the autumn, watch the leaves fall. The simple phenomenon of light
— brightness angling across the air — struck him as a transcendent piece
of good news. (p. 85)

Once at a meeting he had looked out the conference-room window at the yellow gingko leaves and "found his vitality and his intelligence suddenly stimulated and had been able to make a substantial contribution to the meeting founded foursquare on the brightness of leaves" (p. 85). Farragut, like all the characters with whom Cheever most sympathizes, lives in an organic relationship with the natural world. Its importance for him is emphasized in his profound sense of its loss through his incarceration.

There are some other less striking continuities between *Falconer* and Cheever's other work. For one thing, Farragut's drug addiction is prefigured by that of Eliot Nailles in *Bullet Park*. The presence of religion is a continuity, although this novel, as mentioned before, deals with it more directly and carries its potential significance further than the earlier works have. Cheever includes practically no comic set-pieces, like the description of Gertrude in "The Country Husband," for which he is known, probably so as to keep the focus more sharply on Farragut. But every time the Cuckold speaks, we have monologue narratives that can stand alone in their vivid, poignant-comic accounts of life with an unfaithful wife or a two-night stand with a male prostitute. Also, while there is less use of the fortuitous turn of event that occurs so often in his stories, readers are likely to feel that Jody's escape — with the help of the Archbishop of New York — and Farragut's — aided by the fact that the hearse is in the garage for an oil change — are accomplished with minimal difficulty or danger. However, Farragut is not permitted to attempt his excessively easy escape until he has come — through personal growth — to deserve freedom.

That Cheever was entirely aware of what he was about in *Falconer* is indicated by a simple statement he made to one interviewer: "I meant to go as far into darkness as I could in pursuit of radiance or brightness. What I really wanted to write was a radiant, radiant book about incarceration, homosexuality and addiction. I think I succeeded."[9] This remark shows that Cheever intended the setting and the events of the novel to be taken primarily as facts of life rather than as literary metaphors. At the same time, he set out to move Farragut and the reader through these bitter facts of human existence to an affirmation of the human being's power to defeat addiction, to find redeeming love in all human encounters, and to transcend incarceration of all kinds. Cheever has declared the existence of love and honor, loyalty and conscience, in the worlds of his previous work — in impersonal cities, in suburbs which enforce conformity, in families whose members selfishly insist on their own prerogatives more than on loving and understanding solidarity. But nowhere are we more impressed and moved by the survival of those who cherish the values embodied in these perpetual Cheever watchwords than in the world of *Falconer,* a world dramatically different on the surface from any that Cheever had created before, but in fact a world that provides for the apotheosis of the values which have informed John Cheever's work from the beginning.

CHAPTER 9

The Continuing Excellence of John Cheever

I T is often said that America is a country of one-book authors, that many of our writers achieve a spectacular success with a single work which they never again can match, though some have died trying. We all know that this perception applies clearly to some writers, like Stephen Crane and Ralph Ellison, and that it comes uncomfortably close to the truth about Hawthorne, Melville, Whitman, Twain, Fitzgerald, and Hemingway. Even if their readers would insist on a more pervasive excellence in their careers, we know that these writers themselves suffered, openly or obliquely, from a sense of being unable to continue to write at the level of their best work. Furthermore, the list of writers who continued to develop their art over an extended career is short, much shorter than in the English literary tradition. Most would name James, many Faulkner, some Wharton, and after that the names of writers whom we associate with quantity — Cooper, Howells, O'Hara — do not ring a qualitatively high note for us. Consequently, in the light of our literary history and observing in our own time Salinger silent in Vermont, Capote drunk and drugged on television, Mailer caricaturing himself in person and in print, and Vonnegut murdering his characters in a fictional dead-end, we cannot help but take note of the multi-book career, the writer who doesn't rewrite early successes but dares to grow and to try new things.

It is not premature to judge that John Cheever's career belongs with those courageous, extended American literary careers. The publication of *Falconer,* with its shockingly new milieu and its unusually violent language, is only the most dramatic proof that Cheever is not afraid to push off from past accomplishments and to work with previously untried materials. But his whole body of work reveals that he has consistently been willing to grow, to extend the range of his subject matter, and increasingly to complicate his recurring themes. One of his early reviewers worried that the main danger for Cheever might be to find himself trapped within the elegant style of his promising early stories, but Cheever has enlarged and refined that style through four novels and several hundred short stories. No two collections of short stories are the same; some obvious development of theme, tone, or style marks each. Even *The Wapshot Scandal,* a sequel, goes far beyond the setting and the perspective of *The Wapshot Chronicle. Bullet Park* was different enough from Cheever's previous work so as to be radically misunderstood when it was published, and *Falconer* was an even more startling departure from Cheever's earlier subject matter and style.

At the same time, Cheever does have certain recurrent themes which give a sense of coherence to his career, much as the international theme and the conflict between innocence and experience unify the works of Henry James. One of Cheever's most frequently chosen subjects is family relationships, but he is no simple chronicler or analyst. He has too much respect for the mysterious spaces as well as the successful synapses between husbands and wives, parents and children. He also writes of the relationship between brothers, showing it as intimate and loyal in *The Wapshot Chronicle,* as fratricidal in *Falconer,* with many gradations in between in other works. Along with this focus on the family, Cheever incorporates the historical and cultural developments of his times into his fiction. The Depression and World War II figure to some degree in his earliest stories; bomb shelters, the space program, and the sexual revolution appear in his later works. The ground where these dual interests in the internal dynamics of the person and the external convulsions of the world meet is in Cheever's attention to the dailiness of American life, the focus that often gets him characterized as a novelist of manners. Generally, however, in the novel form, he deals with the more extreme experiences of human life; it is more often his stories that really work out the relationships between the inner person and outer world, the present and the past, the best that we dream of being and the compromises we continually make.

Cheever's career is varied enough that it is possible to see links between him and a number of American writers and movements. It seems to me, however, that beneath the realistic surface of most of his novels and stories, beneath the careful delineation of manners, a representational American milieu, and historical and cultural facts, Cheever is basically a romantic and a moralist. He is a romantic in that his interest finally is in the individual. However much he may write about behavior in New England small towns, Eastern big cities, and the American suburb, he is really most concerned about the reverberations of that behavior in the individual human soul. And he is a moralist in that despite the comic texture of his works, the toleration for all manner of human foibles, and the general affirmation which most of his works finally reach, he is always aware of right and wrong, better and worse, life-enhancing and life-diminishing qualities both in people and in the world which can thwart the full humanity of his characters. In these qualities he seems most to resemble James and Fitzgerald. He is like James in his understanding of the interplay between the individual and society, between inner morality and outer manner, and because he can successfully capture that connection in fiction. He is like Fitzgerald in the lyrical elegance of his style and in his use of that style to contain the pain of the perception that the world often frustrates and even destroys the best possibilities of human beings. There is also a little echo of Hawthorne in Cheever's work in his New England moral toughness, his wish that people reach their best human potential despite a lack of cooperation by society. It seems to me that Cheever in his own time has no close peer. He is less naively romantic than Salinger, less simply a chronicler of manners than Auchincloss, less egocentric than Mailer, less narrowly focused than Malamud or Roth, less gimmicky than Vonnegut. His combination of attention to the individual and awareness of the facts and the power of society connect him more with classic American authors like Hawthorne, James, and Fitzgerald; and despite his own New England background and East Coast life-style, he has resisted the post–World War II tendency of American writers to divert American fiction toward a narrow exploration of their own individual religious, racial, or geographical roots.

Yet, at the same time that Cheever's ability to generalize his materials is clear, his readers are becoming more aware of the genesis of those materials out of his own life. This is due mostly to Cheever's increasing willingness to grant interviews despite his well-known shyness and indirection in that situation, the most remarkable evidence of which was his two-night appearance on Dick Cavett's PBS television show in 1978 after the publication of *Falconer*. Consequently, we know more and more about his childhood, his family, his problems with alcohol; and we are more able to consider how his crucial life experiences have entered into his fiction. His very first story, "Expelled," is based directly on his own prep-school expulsion; but even at the age of sixteen, he showed skill at getting beyond the personal vibrations of the experience to a literary presentation of the material. We know also that Cheever's relationship with his brother was intense and troubled, but taken as a group Cheever's stories about brothers reveal such a diverse view of fraternal relations that once again we must conclude that while his own experience may have provoked his interest in the subject, his literary skill transmuted the experience into art. In a recent interview, after revealing that this character or that was indeed based on one family member or another, Cheever commented on the relationship of the writer's experience to his finished work:

It seems to me that any confusion between autobiography and fiction debases fiction. The role autobiography plays in fiction is precisely the role that reality plays in a dream. As you dream your ship, you perhaps know the boat, but you're going towards a coast that is quite strange; you're wearing strange clothes, the language that is being spoken around you is a language you don't understand, but the woman on your left is your wife. It seems to me that this not capricious but quite mysterious union of fact and imagination one also finds in fiction. My favorite definition of fiction is Cocteau's "Literature is a force of memory that we have not yet understood." It seems that in a book that one finds gratifying, the writer is able to present the reader with a memory he has already possessed, but has not comprehended.[1]

This statement is helpful in two ways. For one, it clearly states Cheever's own sense of the relation of memory and experience to his finished works of fiction. For another, it may help explain why Cheever's work so often provokes the reader to a ready acquiescence that life *is* really like that, to frequent shocks of recognition.

The single most remarkable aspect of Cheever's career so far is, I think, the beauty and consistency of his style. It is lyrical without being flowery; it is precise without being coldly analytical. But in good fiction, style is intrinsic rather than an extra element troweled on over plot, character, and setting; it convinces us that it proceeds inevitably from the inner being of the writer. When we are thus convinced, we feel confident in developing a sense of the writer from the quality and nature of the style. I think one can safely, accurately come to just such a sense of John Cheever, and a remark he made recently on the subject of style helps indicate what I mean:

I think one has a choice, with imagery, either to enlarge or to diminish. At this point I find diminishment despicable. When I was a younger man I thought it brilliant. But as a mature novelist I think one's responsibility is to perhaps get a few more details in and come out with a somewhat larger character.[2]

Cheever's great contribution to contemporary American literature is that when he brings his formidable gifts of observation and language to bear upon life in our time, he doesn't diminish it but instead leaves us with a sense of increased possibility and even, at times, joy.

Notes and References

Chapter One

1. *Newsweek,* July 4, 1976, p. 36.
2. *Time to Murder and Create: The Contemporary Novel in Crisis* (New York, 1966), p. 171.
3. Susan Cheever Cowley, "A Duet of Cheevers," *Newsweek,* March 14, 1977, p. 68.
4. Eleanor Munro, "Not Only I the Narrator but I John Cheever...," *Ms.* (April, 1977), p. 76.
5. *Ibid.*
6. Samuel Coale, *John Cheever* (New York, 1977), p. 3.
7. Cowley, p. 69.
8. "Expelled," *New Republic* 64 (October 1, 1930), 174.
9. Cowley, p. 69.
10. *The Way Some People Live* (New York, 1943). Page references are to this edition and appear in parentheses in the text.
11. "Books," *Yale Review* 32 (Summer 1943), xii, xiv.

Chapter Two

1. Cowley, p. 68.
2. Annette Grant, "The Art of Fiction LXII," *Paris Review* 17 (Fall 1976), 53.
3. "Cheever's Triumph," *Newsweek,* March 14, 1977, p. 62.
4. *The Enormous Radio and Other Stories* (New York, 1953). Page references are to this edition and appear in parentheses in the text.
5. Burton Kendle, "Cheever's Use of Mythology in 'The Enormous Radio,' " *Studies in Short Fiction* 4 (Spring 1967), 262.
6. Henrietta T. Harmsel, " 'Young Goodman Brown' and 'The Enormous Radio,' " *Studies in Short Fiction* 9 (Fall 1972), 407–408.
7. *John Cheever,* p. 35.
8. *The American Short Story: Continuity and Change, 1940–1975* (Boston, 1975), p. 32.
9. "Outstanding Novels," *Yale Review* 42 (June 1953), x, xii.

Chapter Three

1. Donald Malcolm, "John Cheever's Photograph Album," *New Republic* 136 (June 3, 1957), 17.

2. Rollene Waterman, "Biographical Sketch," *Saturday Review,* September 13, 1958, p. 33.

3. Grant, p. 48.

4. *The Wapshot Chronicle* (New York, 1957). Page references are to this edition and appear in parentheses in the text.

5. Grant, p. 60.

6. "John Cheever and Comedy," *Critique* 6 (Spring 1963), 76.

7. Grant, p. 47.

8. "The Domesticated Stroke of John Cheever," *New England Quarterly* 44 (December 1971), 542.

9. *The Wapshot Scandal* (New York, 1964). Page references are to this edition and appear in parentheses in the text.

10. "America Aglow," *Commentary* 38 (July 1964), 66.

11. "A Surpassing Sequel," *Book Week,* January 5, 1964, p. 1.

12. Grant, p. 51.

13. *Ibid.,* p. 61.

14. *Ibid.,* p. 56.

15. *Commentary* 38 (July 1964), 67.

Chapter Four

1. "John Cheever and the Charms of Innocence: The Craft of *The Wapshot Scandal,*" *Hollins Critic* I, ii (April 1964), 6.

2. *Bright Book of Life: American Novelists from Hemingway to Mailer* (Boston, 1973), pp. 111–12.

3. *The Housebreaker of Shady Hill and Other Stories* (New York, 1958). Page references are to this edition and appear in parentheses in the text.

4. *Hollins Critic* I, ii (April 1964), 4.

5. *New England Quarterly* 44 (December 1971), 541.

6. *Some People, Places, and Things That Will Not Appear in My Next Novel* (New York, 1961). Page references are to this edition and appear in parentheses in the text.

7. *The American Short Story,* p. 36.

8. Quoted in Herbert Gold, ed. *Fiction of the Fifties* (Garden City, New York, 1959), p. 21.

9. David Ray, "The Weeding-Out Process," *Saturday Review,* May 27, 1961, p. 20.

Chapter Five

1. *The American Short Story,* p. 37.
2. *The Brigadier and the Golf Widow* (New York, 1964). Page references are to this edition and appear in parentheses in the text.
3. Jane H. Kay, "Cheever's Gift for the Ordinary," *Christian Science Monitor,* October 22, 1964, p. 7.

Chapter Six

1. *Fiction of the Fifties,* p. 8.
2. *Ibid.*
3. *John Cheever,* p. 95.
4. "A Grand Gatherum of Some Late Twentieth Century Weirdos," *New York Times Book Review,* April 27, 1969, p. 40.
5. "Recent Novels: The Language of Art," *Yale Review* 59 (Autumn 1969), 111–12.
6. *John Cheever,* pp. 103–105.
7. "The Portable Abyss," *Time,* April 25, 1969, p. 109.
8. "Witchcraft in Bullet Park," *New York Times Book Review,* October 24, 1971, pp. 2, 24.
9. *Bullet Park* (New York, 1969). Page references are to this edition and appear in parentheses in the text.
10. *New York Times Book Review,* October 24, 1971, p. 2.
11. *Ibid.*
12. *Ibid.*

Chapter Seven

1. *"The World of Apples,"* New York Times Book Review, May 20, 1973, p. 1.
2. D. Keith Mano, *"The World of Apples,"* Book World (Washington Post), July 1, 1973, p. 1.
3. *The World of Apples* (New York, 1973). Page references are to this edition and appear in parentheses in the text.

Chapter Eight

1. *Falconer* (New York, 1977). Page references are to this edition and appear in parentheses in the text.
2. *Time to Murder and Create,* p. 177.
3. Munro, p. 77.
4. *Newsweek,* March 14, 1977, p. 62.
5. "View from the Big House," *Time,* February 28, 1977, p. 80.

6. "Crying in the Wilderness," *Harper's,* March, 1977, p. 89.

7. *Ibid.*

8. Perry Meisel, "Cheever's Challenge: Find Freedom," *Village Voice,* March 21, 1977, p. 74.

9. Jan Herman, "John Cheever Never Plays the Celebrity," *Show* (Chicago *Sun-Times*), April 17, 1977, p. 1.

Chapter Nine

1. John Hersey, "John Cheever, Boy and Man," *New York Times Book Review,* March 26, 1978, p. 32.

2. *Ibid.*

Selected Bibliography

PRIMARY SOURCES

1. Novels

Bullet Park. New York: Alfred A. Knopf, 1969. New York: Ballantine, 1978 (paperback).

Falconer. New York: Alfred A. Knopf, 1977. New York: Ballantine, 1978 (paperback).

The Wapshot Chronicle. New York: Harper and Row, 1957, 1973 (paperback).

The Wapshot Scandal. New York: Harper and Row, 1964, 1973 (paperback).

2. Short-Story Collections

The Brigadier and the Golf Widow. New York: Harper and Row, 1964. Includes: "The Brigadier and the Golf Widow," "The Angel of the Bridge," "An Educated American Woman," "The Swimmer," "Metamorphoses," "The Bella Lingua," "Clementina," "A Woman without a Country," "Reunion, "The Chaste Clarissa," "The Music Teacher," "The Seaside Houses," "Just One More Time," "Marito in Città," "A Vision of the World," "The Ocean."

The Enormous Radio and Other Stories. New York: Funk and Wagnalls, Inc., 1953. Includes: "Goodbye, My Brother," "The Pot of Gold," "O City of Broken Dreams," "The Children," "Torch Song," "The Cure," "The Hartleys," "The Summer Farmer," "The Superintendent," "The Enormous Radio," "The Season of Divorce," "Christmas is a Sad Season for the Poor," "The Sutton Place Story," "Clancy in the Tower of Babel."

The Housebreaker of Shady Hill and Other Stories. New York: Harper and Row, 1958. Includes: "The Housebreaker of Shady Hill," "O Youth and Beauty!," "The Country Husband," "The Sorrows of Gin," "The Worm in the Apple," "The Five-forty-eight," "Just Tell Me Who It Was," "The Trouble of Marcie Flint."

Some People, Places, and Things That Will Not Appear in My Next Novel. New York: Harper and Row, 1961. Includes: "The Death of Justina," "Brimmer," "The Lowboy," "The Duchess," "The Scarlet Moving Van," "The Golden Age," "The Wrysons," "Boy in Rome," "A Miscellany of Characters That Will Not Appear."

151

The Stories of John Cheever. New York: Alfred A. Knopf, 1978. 61
    stories from throughout his career.
The Way Some People Live. New York: Random House, 1943. Includes:
    "Summer Theatre," "Forever Hold Your Peace," "In the Eyes of
    God," "The Pleasures of Solitude," "Cat," "Summer Remem-
    bered," "Of Love: A Testimony," "The Edge of the World," "Hello,
    Dear," "Happy Birthday, Enid," "Run, Sheep, Run," "The Law of
    the Jungle," "North of Portland," "Washington Boarding House,"
    "Riding Stable," "Survivor," "Tomorrow is a Beautiful Day,"
    "There They Go," "The Shape of a Night," "The Brothers," "Pub-
    lick House," "When Grandmother Goes," "A Border Incident,"
    "The New World," "These Tragic Years," "Goodbye, Broadway —
    Hello, Hello," "Problem No. 4," "The Peril in the Streets," "The
    Sorcerer's Balm," "The Man Who Was Very Homesick for New
    York."
The World of Apples. New York: Alfred A. Knopf, 1973. New York:
    Warner Books, 1978 (paperback). Includes: "The Fourth Alarm,"
    "The Jewels of the Cabots," "Percy," "Artemis, the Honest Well
    Digger," "The Chimera," "Mene, Mene, Tekel, Upharsin," "Mont-
    raldo," "Three Stories," "The Geometry of Love," "The World of
    Apples."

3. Uncollected Short Stories

"Another Story." *New Yorker* 43 (February 25, 1967), 42–48.
"Autobiography of a Drummer." *New Republic* 84 (October 23, 1935),
    294–95.
"The Beautiful Mountains." *New Yorker* 22 (February 8, 1947), 26–30.
"The Bus to St. James." *New Yorker* 31 (January 14, 1956), 24–31.
"The Common Day." *New Yorker* 23 (August 2, 1947), 19–24.
"The Day the Pig Fell into the Well." *New Yorker* 30 (October 23, 1954),
    32–40.
"Dear Lord, We Thank Thee for Thy Bounty." *New Yorker* 19 (Novem-
    ber 27, 1943), 30–31.
"The Events of That Easter." *New Yorker* 35 (May 16, 1959), 40–48.
"Expelled." *New Republic* 64 (October 1, 1930), 171–74.
"Family Dinner." *Colliers* 110 (July 25, 1942), 62.
"The Folding-Chair Set." *New Yorker* 51 (October 13, 1975), 36–38.
"Frere Jacques," *Atlantic Monthly* 161 (March 1938), 379–82.
"The Habit." *New Yorker* 40 (March 7, 1964), 45–47.
"His Young Wife." *Colliers* 101 (January 1, 1938), 21–22.
"How Dr. Wareham Kept His Servants." *The Reporter* 14 (April 5, 1956),
    40–45.
"In Passing." *Atlantic Monthly* 157 (March 1936), 331–43.
"The International Wilderness." *New Yorker* 39 (April 6, 1963), 43–47.
"The Invisible Ship." *New Yorker* 19 (August 7, 1943), 17–21.

"The Journal of a Writer With a Hole in One Sock." *Reporter* 13 (December 29, 1955), 25–30.

"Keep the Ball Rolling," *New Yorker* 24 (May 29, 1948), 21–26.

"The Loaves, the Lion-fish, and the Bear." *Esquire* 82 (November 1974), 110–11.

"Love in the Islands." *New Yorker* 22 (December 7, 1946), 40–42.

"The Man She Loved." *Colliers* 106 (August 24, 1940), 52.

"Manila." *New Yorker* 21 (July 28, 1945), 20–23.

"The Mouth of the Turtle." *New Yorker* 20 (November 11, 1944), 25–26.

"My Friends and Neighbors All, Farewell." *New Yorker* 19 (October 2, 1943), 23–26.

"Paola." *New Yorker* 34 (July 26, 1958), 22–29.

"People You Meet." *New Yorker* 26 (December 2, 1950), 44–49.

"A Place of Great Historical Interest." *New Yorker* 18 (February 21, 1942), 17–19.

"President of the Argentine." *Atlantic* 237 (April 1976), 43–45.

"The Princess." *New Republic* 88 (October 28, 1936), 345–47.

"Reasonable Music." *Harper's* 201 (November 1950), 58–63.

"Roseheath." *New Yorker* 23 (August 16, 1947), 29–31.

"Saratoga." *Colliers* 102 (August 13, 1938), 12–13.

"Sergeant Limeburner." *New Yorker* 19 (March 13, 1943), 19–25.

"The Single Purpose of Leon Burrows." *New Yorker* 20 (October 7, 1944), 18–22.

"Somebody Has to Die." *New Yorker* 20 (June 24, 1944), 27–28.

"A Tale of Old Pennsylvania." *New Yorker* 19 (May 29, 1943), 20–23.

"The Teaser." *New Republic* 92 (September 1937), 128–29.

"The Temptations of Emma Boynton." *New Yorker* 25 (November 26, 1949), 29–31.

"They Shall Inherit the Earth." *New Yorker* 19 (April 10, 1943), 17–18.

"Triad." *Playboy* 20 (January 1973), 99.

"Trip to the Moon." *Good Housekeeping* 121 (October 1945), 22–23.

"The True Confessions of Henry Pell." *Harper's* 208 (June 1954), 54–61.

"Vega." *Harper's* 199 (December 1949), 86–95.

"A Walk in the Park." *Good Housekeeping* 119 (October 1944), 136–37.

SECONDARY SOURCES

ALDRIDGE, JOHN. *Time to Murder and Create: The Contemporary Novel in Crisis.* New York: David McKay, 1966, pp. 171–77. Focuses on Cheever's handling of contemporary American culture, primarily in *The Brigadier and the Golf Widow.*

AUSER, CORTLAND P. "John Cheever's Myth of Man and Time: 'The Swimmer.' " *CEA Critic* 29 (March 1967), 18–19. Brief analysis of mythic patterns of quest, journey, initiation, and discovery in the story; also invokes the Ulysses story and Ovid's *Metamorphosis.*

154   JOHN CHEEVER

BRACHER, FREDERICK. "John Cheever and Comedy." *Critique* 6, i (Spring 1963), 66–77. Very useful analysis of Cheever's achievement in the short-story form and of the implications of his classical comic outlook.

———. "John Cheever: A Vision of the World." *Claremont Quarterly* 11 (Winter 1964), 47–57. General study of the themes of Cheever's work, with an emphasis on the stories.

BURHANS, CLINTON S., JR. "John Cheever and the Grave of Social Coherence." *Twentieth Century Literature* 14 (January 1969), 187–209. Persuasive and thorough discussion of Cheever's social criticism of the contemporary American scene, particularly in the Wapshot novels and *The Brigadier and the Golf Widow.*

CHESNICK, EUGENE. "The Domesticated Stroke of John Cheever." *New England Quarterly* 44 (December 1971), 531–52. Comprehensive study of Cheever's work through *Bullet Park* which places him within the New England literary tradition.

COALE, SAMUEL. *John Cheever.* New York: Frederick Ungar, 1977 (Modern Literature Monographs), 130 pp. Brief introductory study; good discussion of novels; discusses only selected stories. [Bibliography].

GARRETT, GEORGE. "John Cheever and the Charms of Innocence: The Craft of *The Wapshot Scandal.*" *Hollins Critic* 1, ii (April 1964), 1–12. Thorough and appreciative discussion of *The Wapshot Scandal,* which connects it to the rest of Cheever's work.

GREENE, BEATRICE. "Icarus at St. Botolphs: A Descent to 'Unwonted Otherness.' " *Style* 5 (Spring 1971), 119–37. Stylistic analysis of the Wapshot novels.

HARMSEL, HENRIETTA T. " 'Young Goodman Brown' and 'The Enormous Radio.' " *Studies in Short Fiction* 9 (Fall 1972), 407–408. Argues against Kendle's thesis and proposes instead parallels between Cheever and Hawthorne.

HASSAN, IHAB. *Radical Innocence: Studies in the Contemporary American Novel.* Princeton: Princeton University Press, 1961, pp. 188–94. Brief discussion of *The Wapshot Chronicle.*

HYMAN, STANLEY EDGAR. *Standards: A Chronicle of Books for Our Time.* New York: Horizon Press, 1966, pp. 199–203. Brief discussion of *The Wapshot Scandal.*

KAUFFMANN, STANLEY. "Literature of the Early Sixties." *Wilson Library Bulletin* 39 (May 1965), 748–77. General introduction; briefly compares Cheever's style to Fitzgerald's.

KAZIN, ALFRED. *Bright Book of Life: American Novelists and Storytellers from Hemingway to Mailer.* Boston: Little, Brown, 1973, pp. 110–14. Brief remarks; criticizes Cheever for facile handling of his social themes.

KENDLE, BURTON. "Cheever's Use of Mythology in 'The Enormous Radio.' " *Studies in Short Fiction* 4 (Spring 1967), 262–74. Treats

"The Enormous Radio" as an ironic version of the Edenic myth.

MOORE, S. C. "The Hero on the 5:42: John Cheever's Short Fiction." *Western Humanities Review* 30 (Spring 1976), 147–52. Analyzes the mixture of mimetic and fabulous elements in Cheever's stories.

"Ovid in Ossining." *Time* 83 (March 27, 1964), 66–70. Thorough biographical background; interesting quotations by Cheever.

PEDEN, WILLIAM. *The American Short Story: Continuity and Change, 1940–1975.* Boston: Houghton, Mifflin, 1975, pp. 30–39. Treats the attention to manners in Cheever's short fiction; particularly values *The Brigadier and the Golf Widow.*

2. Major Reviews

The Brigadier and the Golf Widow

KAY, JANE H. "Cheever's Gift for the Ordinary." *Christian Science Monitor,* October 22, 1964, p. 7.

SCULLY, JAMES. "The Oracle of Subocracy." *Nation* 200 (February 8, 1965), 144–45.

Bullet Park

DEMOTT, BENJAMIN. "A Grand Gatherum of Some Late Twentieth Century Weirdos." *New York Times Book Review,* April 27, 1969, pp. 1, 40–41. Negative review that misses the thematic point and the structural justification.

GARDNER, JOHN. "Witchcraft in Bullet Park." *New York Times Book Review,* October 24, 1971, pp. 2, 24. A fine, corrective review which answers unappreciative critics and gives the book a thorough reading.

The Enormous Radio and Other Stories

KELLY, JAMES. "The Have-Not-Enoughs." *New York Times Book Review,* May 10, 1953, p. 21.

MIZENER, ARTHUR. "In Genteel Tradition." *New Republic,* May 25, 1953, pp. 10–20.

PEDEN, WILLIAM. "Esthetics of the Story, New Yorker Type." *Saturday Review,* April 11, 1953, pp. 43–44. Focuses on the phenomenon of the *New Yorker* story as executed by Cheever and others.

PICKREL, PAUL. "Outstanding Novels." *Yale Review* 42 (June 1953), x, xii.

Falconer

CLEMONS, WALTER. "Cheever's Triumph." *Newsweek,* March 14, 1977, pp. 61–67. An excellent study of Cheever's whole career as it culminates in *Falconer;* deft synthesis of biographical and literary data.

LEONARD, JOHN. "Crying in the Wilderness." *Harper's,* March 1977, pp. 88–89.

MEISEL, PERRY. "Cheever's Challenge: Find Freedom." *Village Voice,*
     March 21, 1977, pp. 74, 76. Helpfully complex understanding of the
     novel's religious content.
SHEPPARD, R. Z. "View from the Big House." *Time,* February 28, 1977,
     pp. 79–80.

The Housebreaker of Shady Hill and Other Stories

HICKS, GRANVILLE. "Cheever and Others." *Saturday Review,* September
     13, 1958, pp. 33, 47. Emphasizes the theme of inner vulnerability in
     this collection that on the surface seems to concern itself with
     manners.
PEDEN, WILLIAM. "How Sad It All Is." *New York Times Book Review,*
     September 7, 1958, p. 5.

People, Places and Things

RAY, DAVID. "The Weeding-Out Process." *Saturday Review,* May 27,
     1961, p. 20.
WARNKE, FRANK J. "Cheever's Inferno." *New Republic,* May 15, 1961,
     p. 18. Insightful review of this underappreciated collection; relates
     Cheever to the vision of Hawthorne and Melville; celebrates his style.

The Wapshot Chronicle

BAKER, CARLOS. "Yankee Gallimaufry." *Saturday Review,* March 23,
     1957, p. 14.
ESTY, WILLIAM. "Out of an Abundant Love of Created Things."
     Commonweal 66 (May 17, 1957), 187–88.
MALCOLM, DONALD. "John Cheever's Photograph Album." *New
     Republic,* June 3, 1957, pp. 17–18. Takes the view that the fictional
     elements are not effectively formed into a novelistic whole.

The Wapshot Scandal

CORKE, HILARY. "Sugary Days in St. Botolphs." *New Republic,* January
     25, 1964, pp. 19–21. Very critical of the novel in terms of unity.
JANEWAY, ELIZABETH. "Things Aren't What They Seem." *New York
     Times Book Review,* January 5, 1964, pp. 1, 28.
OZICK, CYNTHIA. "America Aglow." *Commentary* 38 (July 1964), 66–67.
     Finds Cheever too facile a social critic but admires style.
WESCOTT, GLENWAY. "A Surpassing Sequel." *Book Week,* January 5,
     1964, pp. 1, 9. The opposite of Corke's view; finds the novel unified
     and effective.

The Way Some People Live

BURT, STRUTHERS. "John Cheever's Sense of Drama." *Saturday Review,*
     April 24, 1943, pp. 9. Very appreciative; predicts a great future for
     Cheever on the basis of his observational and stylistic skill.

KEES, WELDON. "John Cheever's Stories." *New Republic,* April 19, 1943, pp. 516–17.

SCHORER, MARK. "Books." *Yale Review* 32 (Summer 1943), xii–xiv.

The World of Apples

LEONARD, JOHN. "Cheever to Roth to Malamud." *Atlantic,* June 1973, pp. 112–14. A favorable review that sets forth the plot and stylistic virtues of this collection.

MANO, D. KEITH. *"The World of Apples." Book World (Washington Post),* July 1, 1973, pp. 1, 10.

WOIWODE, L. "The World of Apples." *New York Times Book Review,* May 20, 1973, pp. 1, 26. A helpful review, especially on Cheever's style.

3. Interviews

COWLEY, SUSAN CHEEVER. "A Duet of Cheevers." *Newsweek,* March 14, 1977, pp. 68–73.

GRANT, ANNETTE. "The Art of Fiction LXII." *Paris Review* 17 (Fall 1976), 39–60.

HERSEY, JOHN. "John Cheever, Boy and Man." *New York Times Book Review,* March 26, 1978, pp. 3, 31–32.

LEHMANN-HAUPT, CHRISTOPHER. "Talk with John Cheever." *New York Times Book Review,* April 27, 1969, pp. 41–44.

MUNRO, ELEANOR. "Not Only I the Narrator, But I John Cheever...." *Ms.,* April 1977, pp. 74–77, 105.

NICHOLS, LEWIS. "A Visit with John Cheever." *New York Times Book Review,* January 5, 1964, p. 28.

SHEED, WILFRED. "Mr. Saturday, Mr. Monday, and Mr. Cheever." *Life,* April 18, 1969, pp. 39–40.

WALBRIDGE, E. F. "WLB Biography: John Cheever." *Wilson Library Bulletin* 36 (December 1961), 324.

WATERMAN, ROLLENE. "Biographical Sketch." *Saturday Review,* September 13, 1958, p. 33.

Index